The Voice of the Psalms

The Voice of the Psalms

Studies in One Hundred of the Psalms of David

Marcus Loane

formerly Archbishop of Sydney

Wonderful! Music in the house, music in the heart, and
music also in heaven, for joy that we are here!

(JOHN BUNYAN, *The Pilgrim's Progress*. Words spoken by Mercy
in the 'stately palace' called Beautiful.)

Prayers and praises go in pairs:
They have praises who have prayers.

(ANON.)

CHURCHMAN PUBLISHING LIMITED
of Worthing and Folkestone
1990

The Voice of the Psalms
was first published in this edition in 1990 by
CHURCHMAN PUBLISHING LIMITED
117 Broomfield Avenue
Worthing, West Sussex BN14 7SF

Publisher: Peter Smith

Represented in
Dublin; Sydney; Wellington;
Kingston, Ontario and Wilton, Connecticut

Distributed to the book trade by
Bailey Book Distribution Limited
(*a division of the Bailey and Swinfen Holdings Group*)
Warner House, Wear Bay Road
Folkestone, Kent CT19 6PH

ISBN 1 85093 118 6

Printed in Great Britain by
Hobbs the Printers of Southampton

TO
ALFRED STANWAY
OF WHOM IT MAY BE SAID
THAT IN THE SERVICE OF GOD,
WHATSOEVER HIS HAND FOUND TO DO
HE DID WITH ALL HIS MIGHT.
(Ecclesiastes 9:10)

Contents

CONTENTS

Foreword

*I*T is clear that the Psalms were songs of praise which were set to music. Pipe and harp, trumpet and cymbal, were all part of the Old Testament orchestra. Music is an art which may be valued for its own sake; it may be an end in itself. In that sense, it is one of the many facets that make up the culture of a nation; but that is not the same thing as worship. It may be splendid in its own context, but it is not equivalent to the worship of God 'in the beauty of holiness' (Ps. 96:9). The chief glory of music must be measured in terms of its value as an adjunct to true worship; that is only seen when it is cultivated to draw out a richer strain of adoring wonderment at the greatness and the glory of God. There were numerous directions for the proper use of various instruments for this purpose. The pipe (or flute) and the harp seem to have been the two main musical instruments that accompanied the singers. The pipe was the favourite wind instrument and the harp the favourite stringed instrument in Old Testament tradition. It may be said that both have been combined in what is now described as an organ, and an organ, handled with reverence and dignity, is a noble aid to sober, intelligent, feeling worship of God Most High.

One of the most solemn moments in the earthly life of the Lord Jesus was on the eve of His Passion. He had gathered the Twelve in a room in Jerusalem so that they would share the Passover with its time-honoured ritual. It was during that meal that He surprised them by instituting what came to be known as the Lord's Supper. They saw Him take the bread, give thanks, break it, and give it to them to eat, and they heard Him say: 'This is my body which is given for you' (Luke 22:19). Then they saw Him take the cup, give thanks, and pass it round for them to drink as they heard Him say, 'This is my blood . . . which is shed for many unto remission of sins' (Matt. 26:28). That broken bread was the symbol of His body which would soon be given for them; that crimson wine was the symbol of His blood which would soon be shed for them. All this was done in the silence of an awe that could find no words to tell out what was in their hearts. That silence was broken at length with a hymn of praise as they rose from the table: 'And when they had sung a hymn, they went out unto the mount of Olives' (Mark 14:26). This is the only recorded occasion when we are told that He joined in singing, but it was the custom to conclude the Paschal meal with a Psalm. This would be drawn from a section of the Psalter known as the Hallel (Psalms 115–118), and the final words were memorable: 'O give thanks unto the Lord; for he is good: for his mercy endureth for ever' (Ps. 118:29).

Paul and Silas in the Roman colony of Philippi were suddenly arraigned before the magistrates on the ground that they were causing trouble by teaching customs which it was not lawful for a Roman citizen to observe. They were scourged at the hands of the lictors; many stripes were inflicted on them. Their feet were placed in the stocks and they were shut up in the inmost prison. They must have been in pain and in terrible discomfort; but they were not daunted. 'About midnight Paul and Silas were praying and singing hymns unto God' (Acts 16:25). What did they sing? It must have been one of the Psalms of the persecuted people of God in times of old. Perhaps it was that Psalm of defiant faith and courage: 'God is our refuge and strength, a very present help in trouble'(Ps. 46:1). Or did they choose words of lament which had spoken of the innocent suffering of God's people at the hands of evil-doers? 'Yea, for thy sake are we killed all the day long; we are counted as sheep for the slaughter'(Ps. 44:22). Perhaps it was from this experience that Paul drew the inspiration for a tremendous utterance of faith with this verse from this Psalm at its very centre: 'Who shall separate us from the love of Christ? shall tribulation, or anguish, or persecution, or famine, or nakedness, or peril, or sword? Even as it is written, For thy sake we are killed all the day long; we were accounted as sheep for the slaughter. Nay, in all these things we are more than conquerors through him that loved us' (Rom. 8:35–37).

It is clear that singing was an essential feature of New Testament worship. It was enjoined by Paul on his Gentile converts as one of the activities of a truly Spirit-filled life: 'Be filled with the Spirit; speaking one to another in psalms and hymns and spiritual songs, singing and making melody with your heart to the Lord' (Eph. 5:18b–19; cf. Col. 3:16). They were to share with each other in all the rich varieties of praise; this would provide a true outlet for their deepest feelings in music and worship. It is impossible to give a more precise definition of what was meant by hymns and songs, but there is no question at all as to what he had in mind when he spoke of psalms. This is only one of many indications to the effect that a singing spirit was a primary element in the life of the church. So for example it was natural for the disciples to join 'with one accord' in a spontaneous upsurge of praise when they heard how Peter and John had been discharged by the priests and elders (Acts 4:24). At the close of the first Christian century, Pliny, a cultured pagan, bore witness to the same thing as a common feature of Christian fellowship in Bithynia: humble peasant converts would meet early in the morning and sing a hymn of praise to Christ as God. Such psalmody or hymnody might be without the aid of flute or harp, but that did not matter. All that mattered was the authentic melody of those who sang from the fulness of their own hearts.

It is a lovely fact that psalms and hymns and spiritual songs were so much a part of Israel's worship; and that is nowhere more evident than in the Book of Psalms. In what spirit were the tribes of Israel to make their way to the Tabernacle? 'Enter into his gates with thanksgiving, and into his courts with praise: give thanks unto him, and bless his name' (Ps. 100:4). There were many authors: David and Asaph, Heman and Moses, Solomon and the sons of Korah. There was a wide variety in the circumstances in which they were composed: some were national; others were personal; some were full of exuberant celebration; others were steeped in distress. They touch every chord of thought and feeling: loneliness, suffering, confession, thankfulness. This cannot be better expressed than in the words of an article in *The Illustrated Bible Dictionary*:

> Here are mirrored the ideals of religious piety and communion with God, of sorrow for sin and the search for perfection, of walking in darkness, unafraid, by the lamp of faith; of obedience to the law of God, delight in the worship of God, reverence for the Word of God; of humility under the chastening rod, trust when evil triumphs and wickedness prospers, serenity in the midst of storm.

The heart pours out all its feelings in words that leap all the ages to match our needs today.

It was in the nature of things that the history and heritage of Israel should colour the language and furnish the context; but the poetry and the emotion in which the Psalms are steeped have a universal appeal. The pages that follow are a very simple series of single paragraph studies on a verse or verses taken from a hundred of the one hundred and fifty Psalms that make up the whole Psalter. They owe much to the two-volume commentary in the Tyndale Old Testament series by the Reverend Derek Kidner; I am more than grateful for the rich and varied insights his work affords. I have quoted from the *Revised Version* throughout unless otherwise stated, though not unaware of the many excellent translations available today. It is not surprising to know that various metrical versions have been published, of which the best known and most widely used is *The Psalms of David in Metre according to the Version approved by The Church of Scotland*. There are a few Psalms which have been re-shaped as hymns and have become favourites with all Christians. Isaac Watts and W. Kethe wrote two hymns whose Anglo-Saxon simplicity and monolithic grandeur is still undimmed: 'O God, our help in ages past, Our hope for years to come' (cf. Ps. 90); 'All people that on earth do dwell, Sing to the Lord with cheerful voice' (cf. Ps. 100). The two versions of the Shepherd Psalm are softer and more gentle in tone: 'The Lord's my Shepherd, I'll not want'; 'The King of love my Shepherd is, Whose goodness faileth never'. Nor ought one to forget Coverdale's translation retained in the *Book of Common Prayer*. Sometimes its wording is even more mellow than that in other versions, e.g. 'Be thankful unto him, and speak good of his name' (Ps. 100:3, PBV). And one gem which it would be sad indeed to lose; it may fittingly bring this Foreword to a conclusion: 'Thou hast promised to help me' (Ps. 71:2, PBV).

Psalm 1:1-6

*T*HIS Psalm provides a fine contrast between the God-fearing man and the ungodly. It falls into two halves, with three verses in each, and starts with a beatitude: 'Blessed is the man that walketh not in the counsel of the wicked, nor standeth in the way of sinners, nor sitteth in the seat of the scornful' (1:1). He does not listen to worldly advice, is not a party to evil designs, and will not conform to godless scoffing. Rather his life is ruled by the sober guidance that the Law of God sheds upon his path. 'But his delight is in the law of the Lord; and in his law doth he meditate day and night' (1:2). This is like an echo from the famous charge to Joshua when the mantle of leadership fell on his shoulders (Joshua 1:8). It is also like a herald of the noble summons that would ring through the Psalms in an endless variety of ways (cf. Ps. 19:7-11). Imagery drawn from nature is then employed to enhance the picture. 'And he shall be like a tree planted by the streams of water, that bringeth forth its fruit in its season, whose leaf also doth not wither; and whatsoever he doeth shall prosper' (1:3). This would call to mind the garden in which 'every tree that is pleasant to the sight, and good for food' flourished by the river that flowed from the heart of Eden (Gen. 2:9; cf. Rev. 22:2). The stark contrast follows: as for the ungodly, it is not so. They will be like the chaff when the corn is winnowed; as it is tossed into the air, the grain falls to the ground, but the chaff is blown away (1:4). The stern logic that lies behind that grim picture is made plain in the next decisive utterance: 'Therefore the wicked shall not stand in the judgement, nor sinners in the congregation of the righteous' (1:5). There are only two ways in which men can choose to walk, and the day will come when they must part for ever: 'For the Lord knoweth the way of the righteous: but the way of the wicked shall perish' (1:6).

Psalm 2:7

DAVID was named as the author of this Psalm in the Acts (4:25); it was also cited as 'the second psalm' in another quotation (Acts 13:33). The bold and trenchant vigour of the opening paragraph marks a sense of utter astonishment that the kings of the earth should try to put themselves in array against the Lord and His anointed (2:1–5). This led to a devastating statement of God's purpose: 'Yet I have set my king upon my holy hill of Zion' (2:6). The strong personal emphasis of the pronoun invites a paraphrase: 'But as for me, this is what I have done'. And that led on to the splendid declaration which lies at the heart of this Psalm: 'I will tell of the decree: the Lord said unto me, Thou art my son; this day have I begotten thee' (2:7). The title of sonship had been applied to the angels as a body and to Israel as a nation; but it was never used of an individual in the Old Testament apart from this singular utterance. No doubt its primary reference was to Solomon who as David's son was destined to inherit his crown and kingdom, and in that respect, it simply enlarged the promises which David had received: 'I will be his father, and he shall be my son' (2 Sam. 7:14). But this statement was to appear no less than three times in the New Testament as a mystical reference to Christ Himself. It was quoted by Paul in a way that connects 'this day' with the Resurrection (Acts 13:33; cf. Rom. 1:3–4). Then it was quoted twice in the Epistle to the Hebrews as a witness to the fact that God had confirmed the reality of Sonship in the case of the Lord Jesus by a divine decree (Heb. 1:5; 5:5). The word order in the Greek text and its implicit emphasis helps to mark the unique nature of this Divine Sonship: 'My son art thou, and thou alone; this day have I begotten thee'. That lifts our eyes to the boundless plains of eternity, and to Origen's doctrine of eternal generation. No angel was ever declared to be a son in terms like these; and yet, Son though He was, He was made a little lower than the angels that He might taste death for us all (Heb. 2:9).

Psalm 3:3

*T*HIS is one of fourteen Psalms which have a title, and that title is part of the canonical text of Hebrew Scripture. It is editorial in character and is in the third person. 'A Psalm of David, when he fled from Absalom his son'. David was heart-broken as a result of the rebellion of his favourite son; he was also painfully sensitive to the swelling tide of disloyalty and betrayal. 'Lord', he cried, 'how are they increased that trouble me! many are they that rise up against me'(3:1, AV; 2 Sam. 15:12). He was equally sensitive to the spreading rumour that God had now withdrawn from him the light of His favour. 'Many there be which say of my soul, There is no help for him in God'(3:2; cf. 2 Sam. 16:8). But the revolt of Absalom and the slanders of Shimei taught the conscience-stricken king to seek help just where they said there was no help. He turned from their angry menace to the absolute faithfulness of God. Men might say what they would; but the last word was with the Lord. 'But thou, O Lord, art a shield about me; my glory, and the lifter up of mine head'(3:3). Such words are a lovely illustration of the nobility of his mind both as a man and as a poet. The Psalms often speak of God as a shield, but this is the first verse in which that term occurs. It harks back to the great promise to the patriarch Abraham after his meeting with Melchizedek: 'I am thy shield, and thy exceeding great reward'(Gen. 15:1). That shield was round 'about' David (cf. Job 1:10) as though it were held in the hand of God, and the loss of worldly favour was of little account since God was his glory. David had been forced to flee from Jerusalem; he had wept as he went and had covered his head for shame. 'But thou, O Lord, art... my glory, and the lifter up of mine head'. When the dreadful burden of guilt and grave make me bow in dust and ashes, then, O Lord, draw Thou near; be Thou all my glory, and the lifter up of my head.

Psalm 4:1–8

*I*T must have been evening when this Psalm was composed: David wondered whether he could lie down to sleep and be sure that he would dwell in safety. There was so much in his situation to distract and disturb, and the coming nightfall made it easy to brood on his anxieties. Therefore the Psalm began with an appeal to God that was all the stronger in the light of experience: 'Answer me when I call, O God of my righteousness; thou hast set me at large when I was in distress; have mercy upon me, and hear my prayer' (4:1). God's own character and His covenant with His people were both implicit in this very personal form of address. All that God is in Himself and all that He has pledged Himself to be for us are compressed in that appeal: 'O God of my righteousness'. God had in time past brought David out of all his distress and set him free: would He not now respond to this call and answer this cry? David then glanced briefly at those who had brought him into contempt by slander and falsehood: he would have them know that 'the Lord hath set apart him that is godly for himself', and the same Lord would hear his cry (4:3). Then it was as though his thought turned inward in self-counsel and soliloquy: 'Stand in awe, and sin not: commune with your own heart upon your bed, and be still' (4:4). Paul followed the Septuagint when he quoted the first half of this verse with a remarkable application: 'Be ye angry, and sin not: let not the sun go down upon your wrath' (Eph. 4:26). If our hearts were to stand in awe before the majesty and holiness of God, we would shrink from all that has the nature of sin. If we were to commune less with men and more with God, we would learn what it means to be still in His presence. It was in this serene understanding that the Psalmist found the secret of a quiet heart: 'In peace will I both lay me down and sleep: for thou, Lord, alone makest me dwell in safety' (4:8).

Psalm 5:1-3

*T*HIS Psalm belongs to the morning; it has all the freshness of a new day. It has a marked literary structure with five strophes in which the thought alternates like a pendulum between evident devotion to God and vehement rejection of his enemies. The first strophe was compressed into three verses whose word was clear from the outset: 'Give ear to my words, O Lord, consider my meditation' (5:1). He not only spoke with his voice; he would also muse in his heart. Words alone were inadequate to convey his inmost longings, and he would have the Lord hear the one and weigh the other. But he went still further with an urgent appeal of a kind which he could only describe as the sound of his voice: 'Hearken unto the voice of my cry, my King, and my God: for unto thee do I pray' (5:2). His words might be barely articulate, but there could be no room for doubt behind that cry. There was intense feeling in the declaration of loyalty and devotion with its decided personal emphasis: 'My King, and my God'. Even crowned heads cannot bow too low when in the presence of that King Who is none other than God Himself. Nor was that all. What he had said about that voice and that pledge to pray was caught up in the next verse with a decisive commitment: 'My voice shalt thou hear in the morning, O Lord; in the morning will I direct my prayer unto thee, and will look up' (5:3, AV). It had meant much to lie down to sleep with his heart at peace, knowing that the Lord would make him dwell in safety; now with the first light of dawn he would lift up his heart in prayer that the Lord might be the first to hear his voice in the new day. He would order his thoughts and direct his prayer as one who could ever rely on God to hear, and do, beyond all he might ask or think. He would look up and 'keep watch' (RV) for God's answer like those who wait for the morning in the knowledge that day surely follows the night.

Psalm 6:1-5

*T*HIS is the first of the seven penitential Psalms wrung from the heart of David in deep distress. The first five verses pour out his troubles with repeated and fervent prayer for God's gracious intervention; the last five verses round off his lament with determined and forthright trust in his certain deliverance by God. David knew well enough that sin always calls for rebuke and that sinners deserve to be chastened; but he would that this might not come upon him in divine wrath and anger: 'O Lord, rebuke me not in thine anger, neither chasten me in thy hot displeasure' (6:1). His sense of God's wrath had shaken him to the core of his being and made him cry out in grievous anxiety: 'Have mercy upon me, O Lord; for I am weak: O Lord, heal me; for my bones are vexed' (6:2, AV). He was ailing in health and his very life was threatened. Was God indifferent? 'My soul also is sore vexed: and thou, O Lord, how long?' (6:3). That short broken exclamation was the measure of his distress; 'how long' would God withhold His help? But it paves the way for the prayer which lies at the heart of this Psalm: 'Return, O Lord, deliver my soul: save me for thy lovingkindness' sake' (6:4). Five times in these verses the same direct appeal is heard: 'O Lord'. To whom else could he turn even when he scarcely knew how to pray? If he were to go down to the grave, how could he join in the song of praise (6:5)? So let the Lord return and save him out of all his woes; and let Him do this for the sake of His endless mercies. David would stake his soul on that loving-kindness. He saw it as the sheer goodness of God Who acts towards sinful men in grace rather than in wrath once they drop all their own fancied merit and put their trust in Him alone. That is why his prayer suits the need of all who cry from the depth of their own weakness and look to no other but Him for succour and deliverance.

Psalm 8:3-4

*T*HERE is all the splendour of the truly sublime in the thought and language of this Psalm which begins and ends on that note of high praise: 'O Lord, our Lord, how excellent is thy name in all the earth!' (8:1, 9). Who is this Lord to Whose surpassing excellence the whole earth bears witness? David would lift his eyes to the very heavens where the glory of God was seen as 'a crown on the brow of the sky'.[1] His heart was caught up in a mood of awe and worship as he tried to reflect on the boundless wonder of space in all its height and depth: 'When I consider thy heavens, the work of thy fingers, the moon and the stars, which thou hast ordained' (8:3). Perhaps it was after nightfall since moon and stars replace the sun as the central feature in his meditation. There is indeed a special beauty and noble grandeur in the stillness of night beneath a starlit sky; but the question which it prompted was such as none but a man made in the image of God would be likely to ask: 'What is man, that thou art mindful of him? and the son of man, that thou visitest him?' (8:4). Such a question was no idle speculation; it sprang from a heart in the grip of sheer wonder. Man is no more than a speck on the earth, and the earth is no more than a speck in the sky; and yet the great God of heaven is not only mindful of him, but cares for him as well. Man was made a little lower than the angels, but will be crowned with glory and honour; he was destined to rule the whole created universe, and to have all things put under his feet (8:5-6). But that superb picture of man's ultimate destiny could only be fulfilled in and through that Son of Man Whose incarnation and death, leading to His reign in glory, answer to the Psalmist's vision with hope even for the meanest of men: 'We see Jesus, who was made a little lower than the angels for the suffering of death, crowned with glory and honour; that he by the grace of God should taste death for every man' (Heb. 2:9, AV).

---

[1] F. B. Meyer: *The Psalms*, p. 23.

Psalm 12:6

T HE grave situation which gave rise to this Psalm is clear from the outset. The times were dark, and evil was rampant. David lost no time in words of introduction; he plunged at once into a short, abrupt appeal: 'Help, Lord' (12:1). He looked around, and saw that his allies had gone: '. . . for the godly man ceaseth; for the faithful fail from among the children of men' (12:1). There might be no help from man, but there would be no retreat: he would signal for help, and that help had to come from God. But there was more to tell. Those who could not defeat him by the power of the sword could nevertheless weaken his hands and sap his strength by false propaganda. He was keenly aware of the lies and innuendos, the glib talk and equivocal utterances, of those whose one object was to traduce and destroy his reputation. Rumour and slander were easy enough to set on foot, but they had a terrifying effect on a man who cherished his own integrity (12:2–4). But that cry for help did not go unheard; it met with an 'answering oracle'[1]: 'Because of the oppression of the poor: because of the groaning of the needy, I will arise, says the Lord, and set them in safety from those that snarl after them' (12:5, AAPB[2]). That promise was enough to arm his soul with strength against the subtle and boastful voice of his foes, and its solid value was in total contrast with their shallow and specious lies: 'The words of the Lord are pure words; as silver tried in a furnace on the earth, purified seven times' (12:6). There is no dross, no false mixture, nothing at all that would detract from their sterling value. They are like the finest silver which has passed through the most rigorous crucible; their purity is unalloyed. The Psalm concludes with two verses which confirm the promise of help, but show that the circumstances were still unchanged. But the Psalmist could stand in the certain knowledge that the words of the Lord are as pure as shining silver; their value is beyond human telling.

[1] Derek Kidner: *The Psalms, An Introduction and Commentary*, vol. 1, p. 75.
[2] *An Australian Prayer Book*.

Psalm 13:1-6

*T*HE six verses in this Psalm may be seen as three couplets in which the thought climbs up the steep ascent from near despair to the hilltop of a sure faith. The first couplet reiterates the cry 'how long' no less than four times in short and pointed questions: 'How long, O Lord, wilt thou forget me for ever? how long wilt thou hide thy face from me? How long shall I take counsel in my soul, having sorrow in my heart all the day? how long shall mine enemy be exalted over me?' (13:1–2). His mind was in turmoil; he was grieved and baffled; and it was all compressed into that cry: 'How long?'. The same cry has gone up in all ages from those who find it hard to understand why God has not come to their aid. It was heard at its most poignant in the case of those who had been slain for the Word of God: 'How long, O Lord, holy and true, dost thou not judge and avenge our blood on them that dwell on the earth?' (Rev. 6:10, AV). The next couplet turns from the grief of that lament to the voice of earnest supplication: 'Consider and answer me, O Lord my God: lighten mine eyes, lest I sleep the sleep of death; lest mine enemy say, I have prevailed against him; lest mine adversaries rejoice when I am moved' (13:3–4). David was prepared to argue that the alternatives were such that the honour of God Himself was as much at stake as his own safety. That was enough to make him leap to the final couplet in which confidence and certainty replaced all his early turmoil: 'But I have trusted in thy mercy; my heart shall rejoice in thy salvation: I will sing unto the Lord, because he hath dealt bountifully with me' (13:5–6). David had won through to so sure a trust in the steadfast love of God that he could rejoice in the hope of certain deliverance. He was so sure that God would do more than all he had asked that the only language with which he could conclude was that of joy and praise.

9

Psalm 16:1-11

DAVID poured out his heart in this Psalm of hope and expectation. God would preserve him, for in God he had put his trust, and he avowed his faith in a striking declaration: 'Thou art my Lord: I have no good beyond thee' (16:1-2). He knew that his welfare was not beyond the Lord's control, and what that meant to him was then set out in a succession of bold metaphors: 'The Lord is the portion of mine inheritance and of my cup: thou maintainest my lot. The lines are fallen unto me in pleasant places; yea, I have a goodly heritage' (16:5, 6). Does this look back to those dark days when Saul would have driven him out of that inheritance (cf. 1 Sam. 26:19)? He had been taught to set the Lord always before his face and to rely on Him with such total trust that he could not be shaken (16:8). He could contemplate with calm assurance all that was yet unknown both in this life and in the life to come: 'For thou wilt not leave my soul to Sheol; neither wilt thou suffer thine holy one to see corruption' (16:10). The key to an adequate perception of what was in his mind is found in the words of Peter about the Lord Jesus: 'David saith concerning him' (Acts 2:25). David's saying was then quoted to reinforce the apostolic testimony to the Resurrection (cf. Acts 2:27; 13:35). Resurrection was the final seal on all that the Psalm sought to express: it is only because He lives that the man whose trust is in Him shall live also. Therefore David, looking forward through the lens of inspiration and faith, could sum up all that was in his heart with glorious assurance: 'Thou wilt shew me the path of life: in thy presence is fulness of joy; in thy right hand there are pleasures for evermore' (16:11). The path of life will lead without a break into the joy of the very presence of God and John Newton's words will have their glorious fruition:

> Solid joys and lasting treasure
> None but Zion's children know.

Psalm 17:15

*T*HIS Psalm is an echo of the cry in David's heart at the time of his grievous persecution by Saul. He was like a fugitive in the wilderness, hunted among the rocks and caves of the mountains, scarcely knowing where next to turn. His first concern was to plead his integrity and to open his heart to the searching eye of divine judgement: 'Hear the right, O Lord, attend unto my cry... Thou hast proved mine heart...thou hast tried me, and findest nothing' (17:1-3). That led to a direct appeal for God to spread over him the mantle of His almighty protection: 'Shew thy marvellous loving-kindness, O thou that savest them which put their trust in thee' (17:7). He went on to give a vivid account of his encircling enemies and to pray for their ultimate overthrow (17:8-14). Then with one quick movement of thought, he broke away from that vehement diatribe to lift his eyes beyond all his earthly troubles to the everlasting joy of heaven itself: 'As for me, I shall behold thy face in righteousness: I shall be satisfied, when I awake, with thy likeness' (17:15). Such words are a glorious expression of Old Testament confidence in life beyond the grave; they hint at resurrection as well as immortality. Certainty and serenity were the hallmarks of his faith; he would be 'satisfied' in the sense that he would then have more than enough of God's goodness. He would yet stand in His presence where he would see His Face; he would awake from the sleep of death and would find himself transformed with the divine likeness. So it was in the case of Job who was so sure that with his own eyes he would see the Face of God (Job 19:26-27). So it always is for those who are pure in heart: 'they shall see God' (Matt. 5:8). David would have been at home with the New Testament assurance of that hope of glory: 'Now are we the sons of God, and it doth not yet appear what we shall be: but we know that, when he shall appear, we shall be like him; for we shall see him as he is' (1 John 3:2, AV).

Psalm 18:30

THIS great Psalm was David's song of praise at the end of his struggle with Saul. It is also found, with a few minor variations but with the same historical introduction, in the annals at the close of his life (2 Sam. 22:1–51). David's one great desire was to rejoice in the God Who had heard his cry and had brought him out of all his troubles: 'I love thee, O Lord, my strength. The Lord is my rock, and my fortress, and my deliverer; my God, my strong rock, in him will I trust' (18:1–2). It was the voice of a man who had known overwhelming trouble, whose feet seemed to have touched bottom, who had felt as though the sorrows of death would sweep him away. There had been times when it seemed as though he must drown; but the Lord had brought him out of 'many waters' (18:16). There were moments when he felt as though he were lost in the gloom of midnight; but the Lord had shown him the way: 'For thou wilt light my lamp: the Lord my God will lighten my darkness' (18:28). David did not know the reason why he had been compelled to pass through that bitter struggle, but he did not question the love of God Who had ordained it all. There were indeed things which he had found it hard to undergo, harder still to understand; but his confidence in God remained unshaken. He knew that if he were only able to see through the eyes through which God must see, he would not have chosen differently: 'As for God', he wrote, this God Who has done so much for me, 'his way is perfect' (18:30). There had been no mistakes with God; He was always in control. God knew how his footsteps had so often faltered in the path of obedience: his strength had failed; it was not in him to make his own way perfect. But that was not the whole story: 'For who is God, save the Lord? and who is a rock, beside our God?' (18:31). God had strengthened his hands and made him strong in the day of battle; and the same God would do yet more for him. For this God Whose way is perfect, He it is Who 'maketh my way perfect' (18:32).

Psalm 19:1-14

THERE are two great movements of thought in this Psalm, each of which proclaims the greatness and grandeur of God. In the first part, the whole created universe is seen as a revelation of His glorious majesty (19:1-6); in the next part, God's Word written is seen as a revelation of His absolute perfection (19:7-10). David began with a noble statement which rings down the ages: 'The heavens declare the glory of God; and the firmament sheweth his handywork' (19:1). Day and night are alike in their silent witness: 'There is no speech nor language; their voice cannot be heard' (19:3): yet their sound has gone out to the ends of the earth (19:4; cf. Rom. 10:18). The dawn when night passes into day shows how the whole sky may be likened to a tent for the sun when it comes forth, splendid as a bridegroom and strong as an athlete, to run its course from one end of heaven to the other (19:4-6) Then the mood of the Psalm changes and 'the law of the Lord' is brought into focus (19:7). No less than six separate synonyms, each with its own suitable adjective, are then employed to set out the distinctive character of its divine precepts (19:7-9). 'More to be desired are they than gold, yea, than much fine gold: sweeter also than honey and the honeycomb' (19:10). So the treasures of Scripture, like the wonders of nature, all bear witness to the glory of God and teach men to reflect on what ought to be their response: 'Moreover by them is thy servant warned: in keeping of them there is great reward' (19:11). David was all too well aware of the 'errors' which had marred his life and left a trail of 'hidden faults' in contrast with the sun from whose light nothing is hid (19:12; cf. 19:6). He longed for full deliverance from the presumption and the dominion of sin so that he might walk in God's sight with perfect integrity. Therefore the Psalm moved to a close with the lovely prayer of heartfelt dedication: 'Let the words of my mouth and the meditation of my heart be acceptable in thy sight, O Lord, my rock, and my redeemer' (19:14).

13

Psalm 21:1-4

DEREK Kidner says that the note of joy in this Psalm has the ring of 'a coronation ode or a hymn for a royal anniversary'.[1] It makes one think of Charles Wesley's great hymn:

> Rejoice, the Lord is King!
> Your Lord and King adore!
> Mortals, give thanks, and sing,
> And triumph evermore.

The first seven verses are the king's own address to the Lord; the next five verses are the address of the congregation to the king; and the final verse calls upon God in terms of prayer and praise. It all begins with a jubilant utterance: 'The king shall joy in thy strength, O Lord; and in thy salvation how greatly shall he rejoice!' (21:1). David had voiced words of pregnant appeal in the Psalm that precedes this song: 'The Lord . . . grant thee thy heart's desire, and fulfil all thy counsel' (20:1, 4). That prayer had been heard and answered; the Lord had done far more for him than he could ask or think. 'Thou hast given him his heart's desire, and hast not withholden the request of his lips' (21:2). Those who truly delight in the Lord will find Him ever willing to give them their desire: for to delight in Him is to identify their own desire with His to their supreme content. What had David prayed for with such ardent longing and in what did he now rejoice? 'He asked life of thee, thou gavest it him; even length of days for ever and ever' (21:4). Did this refer to the promise that his house and kingdom were to be 'made sure for ever' (2 Sam. 7:16)? Was it more in line with the great farewell words of Moses: 'He is thy life, and the length of thy days' (Deut. 30:20)? It matters little; the words demand the widest compass. 'The last words of David' (2 Sam. 23:1) were to include the grand declaration of faith: 'Verily my house is not so with God; yet he hath made with me an everlasting covenant, ordered in all things, and sure: for it is all my salvation, and all my desire' (2 Sam. 23:5). God had given him length of days; and He would grant him life for evermore.

[1] Kidner, *ibid.*, vol. 1, p. 103.

Psalm 22:1

*N*OTHING in the life of David was so grievous or so tragic that it could not help but evoke that bleak cry of utter desolation: 'My God, my God, why hast thou forsaken me?' (22:1). The whole Psalm is steeped in haunting sorrow, and this cry most of all. But its inner meaning was shrouded in obscurity until it was wrung from the heart of the Son of Man on the cross. Then it rang out of the darkness to lay bare His inmost anguish: 'Jesus cried with a loud voice, saying, Eli, Eli, lama sabachthani?' (Matt. 27:46). It was unique as the only saying on that day to have been preserved in the very language in which it was spoken. But the original Aramaic, and its parallel translation into Greek, and from Greek into English, have all left an echo of awe and terror that time can never efface. It remains mysterious; it defies analysis, it is fraught with a sense of woe. Who can ever probe the depths of that one word *why*? It sums up the cry of all the ages when men have felt totally overwhelmed; they long to know *why* they should have been caught and crushed in the toils of pain and sorrow. But there is no human sorrow like unto His sorrow; then *why* should He of all men have been made to feel as though He had been left in the lurch by God? We can only stand on the edge of that sorrow as we try to grasp its meaning, but there are some facts which we can dimly discern as part of the answer. He Who knew no sin was being made sin for us; therefore He was not spared until He had endured all that sin must entail. The last result of sin is to shut man's soul out from the presence of God; and it was that sense of separation that led to this startling crisis. The guilt of our race and the curse of the law had been laid on his head, and it was more than He could bear. That one stark solitary cry, as though His heart would break, was wrung from His lips: 'My God, my God, *why* hast thou forsaken me?' (Matt. 27:46). But there was a purpose. He was forsaken that we might be forgiven.

Psalm 23:6

Dᴀᴠɪᴅ, the poet and minstrel of Israel, poured out his heart in Psalms full of lyric beauty and tender feeling, haunting rhythm and human pathos. Many of them reflect the life of the lad who had been taken from the sheepfolds to become the king of Israel (cf. 78:70). He had grown up on the moorlands of Bethlehem where from time immemorial shepherds had kept watch over their flocks. It was wild and gaunt country that would breed manliness and would mould character; country where he had slain the lion and the bear as well as sung the songs of Zion. It had coloured his mind just as it had strengthened his arm, and his experience of its realities was the background for much of his imagery. This is never more evident than in the case of this Psalm. It is so fresh in spirit and so free from the sound of strife that it seems to belong to the days of his youth when his heart was full of wonder and faith. He was so sure that the Lord was his shepherd; he would not want. The Lord would lead him in and out, and would guide his footsteps in paths of peace. Goodness and mercy would follow him right on to the end; then he would lift up his eyes to that fold which stands on the hills of God. If goodness and mercy were to follow him all the days of his life, why should he fear the final shadows of death? He would pass through that dark valley to dwell in the house of the Lord for ever. David's great desire in later life was that he might be allowed 'to build an house for the name of the Lord, the God of Israel' (2 Chron. 6:7). That was not to be, though it was well in that it had been in his heart. But there was a house on the farther side of Time in which he would dwell with joy everlasting. Would we know more of that house and what it means? One greater than David has made it plain. It is the 'Father's house' where Jesus Himself has gone; and that is where He would have us be (John 14:2-3).

Psalm 24:1-10

*T*HIS great choral hymn may have been composed at the time when the Ark was brought up by David to its true home on Mount Zion: and all Israel was there 'with sound of the cornet, and with trumpets, and with cymbals, sounding aloud with psalteries and harps'(1 Chron. 15:28). The two verses with which the Psalm opens may have been sung by all the tribes as the festival procession began (24:1-2). Then a single voice may have rung out with the lead question: 'Who shall ascend into the hill of the Lord? and who shall stand in his holy place?'(24:3). The choir would make reply, and the tribes would add their Amen (24:4-6). The whole great host as it neared Mount Zion would then lift up their voice in the sublime demand: 'Lift up your heads, O ye gates; and be ye lift up, ye everlasting doors: and the King of glory shall come in'(24:7). Those who were stationed within the gates would answer with the challenge: 'Who is the King of glory?'. And the crowd would thunder in turn: 'The Lord strong and mighty, the Lord mighty in battle'(24:8). Both the demand and the challenge would be rehearsed again, and the final shout of triumphant assurance would end the song: 'The Lord of hosts, he is the King of glory'(24:9-10). Such a Psalm might have been employed at the time of David's coronation, and it has been deservedly applied to the Ascension from the brow of Olivet The Lord Jesus stood in the midst of that little band of devoted disciples, lifted up His nail-scarred hands, and blessed them; in the very act of blessing, He began to ascend, and they followed Him with wondering eyes until a cloud received Him out of sight. What then? Did not the whole angel host come to meet Him with shouts of acclamation, and to form the escort for His return to the glory of His Father's presence? Did not the gates of that celestial city lift up their heads, and were not the everlasting doors thrown open so that the King of glory might come in? For Who is the King of glory? It is the Lord, even Jesus, Who died, and rose again, and Who is now enthroned at the right hand of God Most High.

Psalm 25:6-7

*T*HIS Psalm belongs to a group whose framework is that of an acrostic based on the letters of the Hebrew alphabet. This was a mnemonic device, an aid to memory, which would be of value for singers and congregation alike. David composed the Psalm in a mood of subdued, but patient, faith, waiting upon God for help and deliverance. There was the ever-present threat from cruel enemies (25:1-3); there was the always urgent need for fresh direction (25:4-5). But there was yet another element, more personal, more insistent: this was the heavy burden of guilt from which he yearned to be set free (25:6-7). David would plead his cause in terms that were meant to put God in mind of His eternal covenant: 'Remember, O Lord, thy tender mercies and thy lovingkindnesses; for they have been ever of old' (25:6). David's appeal to loving-kindness and tender mercy made use of a favourite conjunction of words and ideas, and he could argue from long experience that they were the hallmarks of God's dealings with him. Let God remember His steadfast love; but let Him not remember His servant's sin: 'Remember not the sins of my youth, nor my transgressions: according to thy lovingkindness remember thou me, for thy goodness' sake, O Lord' (25:7). There was total contrast between the sins of youth and the goodness of God; it would be all of grace if God were to bear in mind His goodness rather than the ugly stain of a young man's sin. 'For thy name's sake, O Lord, pardon mine iniquity, for it is great' (25:11). Any man, in any age, like Samuel Rutherford, may find himself standing in the shoes of David, making David's plea his own, and finding the goodness and mercy of God more than equal to all his need:

> With mercy and with judgement
> My web of time he wove:
> And aye the dews of sorrow
> Were lustred with His love.

Psalm 27:1

*T*HIS Psalm may well have been composed during David's exile on account of Absalom's rebellion. He was threatened by the unscrupulous men who followed the arch-rebel and he had been driven to seek safety in a neighbour country beyond Jordan. It was from that place of exile that his eyes were ever turning towards Jerusalem where God had His sanctuary. It was not so much his throne as the shrine which held the Ark for which he longed. The one thing he desired and was resolved to seek was that he might dwell in the house of the Lord all the days of his life. It was with this longing in his heart that he voiced his own ardent declaration of faith: 'The Lord is my light and my salvation; whom shall I fear? the Lord is the strength of my life; of whom shall I be afraid?' (27:1). David had been under acute pressure in his early life when exposed to Saul's persecution; he was under a still graver threat in later life from Absalom's rebellion. But he could turn from the inveterate hostility of such human foes to One Who never failed him. The Lord was the light of his soul and the strength of his life. He shone when all else was dark and troubled, and He gave strength when all else was ready to crumble in ruin. He was the secret of salvation when all others were the authors of confusion. What then? Who was there whom he ought to fear, and what was there that should make him afraid? Such words were a luminous expression of his unswerving confidence in the goodness of God, nor could anything shake his loyalty. That was the kind of faith which had taught him to hold on at all costs and in spite of all appearances. He would have lost heart had he not believed that he would see the goodness of the Lord in the land of the living. Therefore he would conclude with words of self-exhortation to brace his faith: 'Wait on the Lord: be strong, and let thine heart take courage; yea, wait thou on the Lord' (27:14).

Psalm 29:4

*T*HERE is sweeping splendour in the movement of this Psalm from heaven to earth (29:1–2), in the march of the storm from north to south (29:3–9) and in 'the final transition from nature in uproar to the people of God in peace' (29:10–11).[1] The two verses at the head of this Psalm are an address to the first-born sons of light who stand above the tumult of earth and sky, and who are called upon to worship the Lord in the majesty of His holiness (29:1–2). Then the blast and fury of the storm bursts through the restraints of a poet's language. No less than six times 'the voice of the Lord' is heard in the storm. There was first the low and distant sound of thunder as it rumbled over the sea where the storm had begun (29:3–4). Then it struck the cedars on Mount Hermon, and each peal of thunder was reinforced by the lightning that streaked across the sky (29:4–7). It swept down the full length of the country until it was lost in the desert of Kadesh. The cattle were stricken with terror; forests were stripped naked. But those who heard the voice of the Lord as He rode on the wings of the storm could only respond with a cry of worship: 'Every thing saith, Glory' (29:8–9). The Psalm draws to a close with its final picture of the Lord as the One Who is 'king for ever' and 'will bless his people with peace' (29:10–11). But in all the grandeur of vast natural convulsion; in the roar of thunder and the flash of lightning; in the might and majesty of the God of creation, let one phrase sink into our minds and teach us to bow low before Him in worship: 'The voice of the Lord is full of majesty' (29:4).

> O Lord my God, when I in awesome wonder
> Consider all the worlds Thy hands have made;
> I see the stars, I hear the rolling thunder,
> Thy power throughout the universe displayed:
> Then sings my soul, my Saviour-God, to Thee:
> How great Thou art! How great Thou art!

---

[1] Kidner, *ibid.,* vol. 1, p. 125.

20

Psalm 31:5

*T*HIS Psalm sounds the depths of unusual grief in David's experience, but it also climbs the heights of sublime trust in the Lord. It spoke of God as his rock and house of defence, his fortress and stronghold, the One Who had saved him from the net spread by his enemies (31:1–4). David had in mind those days of peril when he had been hunted from place to place by Saul, and had found strength in the knowledge that God Himself was the reality behind all his hiding places. Therefore it was in the Lord that he put his trust, a fact which was finely expressed in the simple declaration of his ultimate confidence both in life and in death: 'Into thine hand I commend my spirit: thou hast redeemed me, O Lord, thou God of truth' (31:5). Those words breathe the serenity of decision and confidence: he was content to yield himself into the Lord's keeping; for he had been redeemed by the Lord God of truth. This prayer was caught up by the Lord Jesus at the very moment of death and was reframed in terms that were appropriate for Him to use: 'Father', He said, 'into thy hands I commend my spirit' (Luke 23:46). He had passed through a whole world of pain and sorrow, but had emerged at last into the calm sunlight of His Father's presence. It lit up His transit through the shadows of death with that peace which passes human understanding. He had known what it was to be in the cruel and implacable hands of Jew and Gentile: they had done their worst; there was no more they could do. But now He would commend Himself into the hands of a loving Father: He knew that those hands are always strong and gentle; they would receive and bear up His human spirit as it passed from earth to heaven. The prayer that brought strength and comfort first to David, then to Jesus, has found an echo in the hearts of saints and martyrs all down the ages. It helps to draw the sting and take the fear out of death; it points to the secret of all Christian fortitude in the hour of dying.

Psalm 32:1–2

*T*HIS Psalm is the second of the seven penitential Psalms ascribed to David, but it differs from the others in that it sets out his experience after he had found the secret of forgiveness and acceptance. The first words told of his profound relief and set the tone for all that would follow: 'Blessed is he' (32:1; cf. 1:1). The blessedness of forgiveness never seems so sweet as when it comes to a man who has struggled to carry on unforgiven. That was how it had been in the case of David. He had remained silent as long as he could, but day and night the hand of God had pressed on his conscience. It was only when he felt that he could resist no more that he had been ready to make a clean breast of his sin. Godly sorrow would mingle with profound relief when at last he heard the words of Nathan: 'The Lord hath put away thy sin' (2 Sam. 12:13). This Psalm was his heartfelt response to that word of divine grace and mercy: 'Blessed is he whose transgression is forgiven, whose sin is covered. Blessed is the man unto whom the Lord imputeth not iniquity' (32:1–2). Several metaphors were called upon to express the complex nature of wrong-doing. It was transgression, the act of a man who crossed the boundary defined by God's Law. It was sin, the moral failure of a man who missed the mark prescribed in that law. It was iniquity, the act of a man who had deviated from the straight and narrow path which that law marked out. But now the guilt of that transgression had been removed; the stain of that sin had been put out of sight; and the folly of that wayward spirit was no longer reckoned to his account. David's sin was to leave an indelible scar on his reign and in his home; but the forgiveness that followed his confession will never be forgotten by the penitent in heart (cf. 32:5). Perhaps that lends added significance to Paul's choice of this Psalm as an illustration of how God will treat as righteous the man who trusts in Him (Rom. 4:6–8). Oh, the blessedness of such a man!

Psalm 34:5

*T*HIS Psalm was the delighted utterance of joyous and grateful relief. It was identified with an experience which had threatened to cost David his life, and it was in the form of an acrostic in which each verse except the last began with a letter of the Hebrew alphabet: 'I will bless the Lord at all times: his praise shall continually be in my mouth'(34:1). He would praise God even when others saw little for which to join in praise, and he would call upon others to share with him in that gladness of heart: 'O magnify the Lord with me, and let us exalt his name together'(34:3). But there are no words in this Psalm which so perfectly reproduce what was in his heart as the words which speak of those whose eyes are fixed on Him: 'They looked unto him, and were lightened'(34:5). Better still is another translation: 'They looked unto him, and were radiant'(cf. Isa. 60:5). Such words may look back to the experience of Moses when he came down from the mount where he had communed with God face to face as a man with his friend: 'Moses wist not that the skin of his face shone while he talked with him' (Ex. 34:29, AV). They may also remind us of what was written about the Lord Himself on that other mountain: 'He was transfigured before them: and his face did shine as the sun'(Matt. 17:2). In the case of Moses, it was reflected glory; it came from his face-to-face communion with God. In the case of Jesus, it was inherent glory; it came from the natural outshining of His divine nature. David spoke of those who were like Moses: 'they looked unto him, and were radiant'. Such a joyous spirit, such a shining face, such radiance in fellowship with God, were the marks of a man whose prayer was heard and who had found that 'the angel of the Lord encampeth round about them that fear him' (34:7). It was for that reason that his eager, thankful, rejoicing gratitude led him to call on all who would hear to put it to the proof for themselves: 'O taste and see that the Lord is good: blessed is the man that trusteth in him'(34:8; cf. 1 Pet. 2:3).

Psalm 35:3

*T*HERE are few points of light in the murky environment which this Psalm calls to mind. David was hedged in by relentless enemies, perhaps sooled on by Saul, and cried out for divine succour lest he should be destroyed: 'Strive thou, O Lord, with them that strive with me: fight thou against them that fight against me' (35:1). Let the Lord stand up for his help, and bar the way against those who were so hot in pursuit (35:2–3). But that urgent appeal for help only reached its climax with his great *cri du coeur*: 'Say unto my soul, I am thy salvation' (35:3). It is a cry that we may well transfer from the field of earthly conflict and apply to spiritual realities. Each of us stands in need of a direct and particular saying of God to our own soul in terms of that magnificent reassurance: 'I am thy salvation'. There is indeed such a thing as an express revelation of the grace and goodness of God: 'He that believeth on the Son of God hath the witness in him' (1 John 5:10). It is as though there were a voice, unheard by the outward ear, yet perfectly audible in the inmost region of his being, that tells a man that God is his mighty Saviour. That is crystal clear in Paul's great declaration: 'The Spirit himself beareth witness with our spirit, that we are children of God' (Rom. 8:16). Such a distinctive utterance in a man's soul is an infallible witness to the love that God has for him. It may be as hard to express in words how this takes place as it is to explain why God should care for such a man at all. But for David, it was as though a gleam of light were to stab through the darkness; he came to feel that his cry would not go unheard: 'My soul shall be joyful in the Lord: it shall rejoice in his salvation' (35:9). Am I no more than a struggling sinner? Am I almost submerged by the powers of darkness? Then let me learn to call upon God like David. Tell me the thing I long to know; make thy voice heard in my inmost spirit. 'Say unto my soul', O Lord God Almighty: 'I, even I, am thy salvation'.

Psalm 36:5–10

*T*HIS Psalm begins and ends with the direst picture of all who work iniquity (36:1–4, 11–12); but the middle section shines like sunlight in its testimony to the unchangeable character of God (36:5–10). David availed himself of the immensities in the world of nature in order to depict His greatness and goodness. Look up to the heavens and search the skies; turn to the strength of the mountains and the depth of the seas: we can neither scale those heights nor plumb those depths; we will never count the last of the stars, nor see the hills crumble and fall. But with all their grandeur, heavens, mountains, skies and seas are inadequate as a picture of the faithfulness and the righteousness of God. 'Thy lovingkindness, O Lord, is in the heavens; thy faithfulness reacheth unto the skies. Thy righteousness is like the mountains of God; thy judgements are a great deep' (36:5–6). The world may be darkened with sin, but God provides for man and beast alike; and such a thought evokes a fresh exclamation of wonder and worship: 'How precious is thy lovingkindness, O God! and the children of men take refuge under the shadow of thy wings' (36:7). The imagery is softened and brought down to the haunts and homes of men. It is as though we were to find ourselves in an Eden of safety and plenty where we may drink from the river of life and walk in the light of God's presence (36:8–9). David's deepest longing then found vent in his prayer: 'O continue thy lovingkindness unto them that know thee; and thy righteousness to the upright in heart' (36:10). The whole Psalm has endless comfort for the man who is poised between the workers of iniquity and the boundless mercies of God. What a superb encouragement lies in those words: 'Thy faithfulness reacheth unto the clouds' (36:5, AV). For the very clouds are only 'the dust of his feet' (Nahum 1:3).

Psalm 37:4

THIS well-loved Psalm is in the form of an acrostic 'with a fresh letter of the Hebrew alphabet to introduce each double verse'.[1] It seems to have sprung straight from the heart of David, and it reflects his own lifelong experience of the goodness of God. He had been young and now he was old; but he did not grow old as those who are worn out with the burden of age. He had remained light of heart and young in spirit. Mature observation of God's dealings with man had taught him the awful folly of the wicked, even though for a time they seem to prosper; and the final comfort of the godly, even though for a time they have to suffer. It will be seen at last that the steps of a good man are ordered by the Lord and that the end of that man is peace. This was all an unconscious reflection of his own walk with God. The first verses are the telling application of the lessons he had known from his days as a shepherd, and they have a simple refrain: 'Fret not thyself' (37:1, 7, 8). Would that sound unduly negative? The word itself suggests something that wears away the mind. Are there no adequate remedies? There are indeed; they are explained in a golden series of quiet instructions. We must learn to trust in the Lord; delight in the Lord; commit our way to the Lord; rest in the Lord; and wait for the Lord (37:3-7). We may choose one verse and let it stand for them all: 'Delight thyself also in the Lord; and he shall give thee the desires of thine heart' (37:4). There will never be a conflict between our more human desires and God's will for our lives if we truly learn to delight in Him. He may ask us as He once asked Simon Peter: 'Lovest thou me more than these?', that is, more than all these others things in your life (John 21:15)? To love Him first and most of all is to delight in Him; and to delight in Him means that all His desires will become our desires; and then He will delight to give us the desires of our own heart.

[1] Kidner, *ibid.*, vol. 1, p. 148.

Psalm 39:7

DAVID was a man of great strength in personal character and national achievement; but there were strands of need and weakness which taught him to rely on God alone. 'Lord', he prayed, 'make me to know mine end, and the measure of my days, what it is; let me know how frail I am' (39:4). He had come to see that a long life in this world was the merest hand-breadth when measured by eternity and that his age was as nothing in God's judgement. Therefore all his inmost feelings were roused to find a voice in prayer: 'And now, Lord, what wait I for? my hope is in thee' (39:7). That was a confession of faith as well as of hope, and it was couched in the simplest imaginable language. There are only twelve words in the English translation, and not one word has more than one syllable. When a man finds himself at the end of his strength and in need of a grasp that is stronger than his own, what else is there to wait for? His hope must be in God, or he will have no hope. It was that hope with its anchor in God Himself which must be seen as the turning point in this Psalm. The sky might still be dark, but there was a break in the clouds. David was an Old Testament figure, but his words are equally true for New Testament people. Our hope for the forgiveness of sin and for acceptance with God, our hope for life now and life in the world to come, a hope that will transcend all the narrow limitations of brevity and frailty in our mortal experience, must be centred in the God of hope Whose only Son died and rose again as the ever-living Saviour of all who trust in Him. It was his firm grasp of this truth that led Paul to speak of 'good hope through grace' (2 Thess. 2:16). The sure comfort of that hope is more than able to shed its light in the darkest hour of need or sorrow. What more do I wait for? is not my hope, O Lord, in Thee?

Psalm 40:7–8

*T*HIS Psalm commemorates David's deliverance from some major peril. It is described in the kind of picture language which serves to veil particular details and so can be applied to all kinds of ugly situations. He had waited long for the Lord Who at last had heard his cry and answered his prayer: 'He brought me up also out of an horrible pit, out of the miry clay; and he set my feet upon a rock, and established my goings' (40:2). David had been rescued from the desolation of a pit as Joseph had been (Gen. 37:28) or from the horror of the mire as Jeremiah would be (Jer. 38:13). He had now found a sure foothold on the solid rock of divine mercy and the Lord had put a new song in his mouth. How could he express his overflowing joy and thankfulness? No mere ritual sacrifice would be welcome; he could offer nothing less than himself. 'Then said I, Lo, I am come; in the roll of the book it is written of me: I delight to do thy will, O my God; yea, thy law is within my heart' (40:7–8). The sonorous dignity and majestic assurance that lie behind these words match the Messianic significance which was ingrained in their content. The roll of the book and the law in his heart were one and the same; they are only mentioned as a parenthesis while the central thought stands out in letters of light: 'Then said I, Lo, I am come. . . I delight to do thy will, O my God'. This is explained in a great New Testament quotation in terms of the voluntary obedience of Christ and His unique self-offering: 'Wherefore when he cometh into the world, he saith, Sacrifice and offering thou wouldest not, but a body didst thou prepare for me. . . Then said I, Lo, I am come (in the roll of the book it is written of me) to do thy will, O God' (Heb. 10:5–7). It was only in His human body that the ultimate offering could be made in the way that the words of David sought to convey; and that supreme self-offering was the one all-sufficient 'sacrifice for sins for ever' (Heb. 10:12).

Psalm 41:9

THIS Psalm has the retrospective value of a man who had passed through great tribulation, but who had found deliverance through God's mercy. It is in the middle verses that he chiefly relived that grim time of trouble (41:4–10), and the climax was reached in words of the utmost pathos: 'Yea, mine own familiar friend, in whom I trusted, which did eat of my bread, hath lifted up his heel against me' (41:9). Who had been so close to David that he could be described in such terms of anguish? It must have been Ahithophel on whose counsel David had relied as though it were 'the oracle of God' (2 Sam. 16:23). The most sacred ties of friendship had been ruptured when Ahithophel threw in his lot with Absalom; he had acted like a vicious mule in lifting up his foot to kick the man who had been his friend as soon as he was down. All that David suffered from that false but once familiar friend was to be re-enacted in the case of the Lord Jesus. He would quote these very words in connection with His betrayal (John 13:18). He had arranged for a room in which to share the Paschal meal with the Twelve: it was in that Passover atmosphere that He planned to convey to them what His death on the cross would mean. But they were still totally unprepared for the appalling announcement at the outset: 'Verily I say unto you, One of you shall betray me, even he that eateth with me' (Mark 14:18). All the Gospels make it clear that He knew that He would be betrayed; Mark in particular was at pains to point out that the man in question was there with Him at the table. Did the disciples understand what He meant when He said that He would be betrayed? It does not seem likely; but the word was dark and ugly. Who would do such a thing? The Lord had in mind the tragic words of David. It would be a man who was His friend; who was close to His heart; who was at that moment a guest at His table. That was Ahithophel in the case of David; but which of the Twelve was like him?

Psalm 42:1-2

*T*HIS Psalm is marked by the sad and wistful refrain of a man whose soul was cast down, but whose faith and hope were unalterably fixed in God Himself. The first words call up the picture of a stricken deer in a time of dearth or a hunted stag in the heat of chase, panting for some cool stream to slake its thirst. Such a picture was a perfect mirror of what he felt in the inmost region of his spirit: 'As the hart panteth after the water brooks, so panteth my soul after thee, O God. My soul thirsteth for God, for the living God: when shall I come and appear before God?' (42:1-2). That cry of *when* showed how vulnerable he was to those who mocked him with the taunt, '*Where* is thy God?' (42:3, 10). But that troubled him far less than his thirst for God Himself, the God Who lives beyond the reach of death and change. A day in the desert, beneath the sun's burning glare, would create a thirst with all the pains of near madness. But this was thirst of a different character; this was the thirst of a soul on fire with longing for God Himself. It seems impossible to read such words without thinking of the cry from the cross: 'Jesus... saith, I thirst' (John 19:28). It was as though all the pains of death were absorbed in a single current and the protracted suffering of nerves and limbs was all expressed in one brief cry:

> His are the thousand sparkling rills
> That from a thousand fountains burst,
> And fill with music all the hills:
> And yet, He saith, I thirst.

But He longed for more than water to cool His lips; He was athirst for God. The joy of His Father's presence had been withheld in the hours of darkness, and that thirst told of a drought in the land where God was not. That was a thirst which no earthly stream could assuage; it was soul-thirst which the comfort of God's presence alone could quench. Then tell me, O my soul, dost thou have such a thirst for God, the living God? He stands before thee still, and thou mayest hear His gracious invitation: 'If any man thirst, let him come unto me, and drink' (John 7:37).

Psalm 43:1–5

*T*HIS Psalm stands in intimate connection with its predecessor; they read like the 'two parts of a single close-knit poem'.[1] The same bitter lament and the same sad refrain are found in the same words in each of them. The voice of the singer is heard from his place of exile in a moving appeal: 'Judge me, O God, and plead my cause against an ungodly nation' (43:1). This was a cry for God to plead his cause and to uphold him in spite of the most hostile criticism. He would assert his faith in God as the God of his strength, and on that ground tried to argue: 'Why go I mourning because of the oppression of the enemy?' (43:2; cf. 42:9). The tone suddenly grew more personal and more intimate; he began to entreat the Lord to cause His light to shine in the darkness of his spiritual uncertainty: 'O send out thy light and thy truth; let them lead me: let them bring me unto thy holy hill, and to thy tabernacles' (43:3). He longed for light so that he could see with perfect vision; he longed for truth so that he could act with perfect integrity. Such a prospect was in itself enough to teach him to speak of God as 'God, my God' (43:4). There may have been no change as yet in his outward circumstances, but that 'exceeding joy' had broken through the storm-clouds with a reassurance which turned strains of lament into words of triumph. 'Why art thou cast down, O my soul? and why art thou disquieted within me?' (43:5; cf. 42:5, 11). His hope was stayed on God Who would send out His light and His truth to guide and lead him. They would brighten his path to the hill of Zion and the altar of God. Therefore he would repeat for the third time the words which had braced and buoyed up his soul: 'For I shall yet praise him, who is the health of my countenance, and my God' (43:5; cf. 42:5, 11).

---

[1] Kidner, *ibid.*, vol. 1, p. 165.

Psalm 44:1

THIS Psalm was an urgent appeal at a time of serious national distress; there were mingled strains of faith and anguish in its moving address to the God of Israel. It was faith that prevailed as it began with the striking recollection of what God had wrought in times past: 'We have heard with our ears, O God, our fathers have told us, what work thou didst in their days, in the days of old' (44:1). They were the heirs of a glorious tradition which could trace God's dealings with them from the very origins of their race at the time when God called Abraham in Ur of the Chaldees. These were things 'which we have heard and known, and our fathers have told us' (78:3). They had passed from father to son down the stream of time from 'the days of old, the years of ancient times' (77:5). It was not folk-lore; it was not legend; nor was it the story of a race of heroes. There had been ever-memorable events as in the passage of the Red Sea, but it was God Who had acted on their behalf. There had been truly magnificent exploits as in the battle of Beth-horon, but it was God Who had nerved their arms with strength. The history and memory of these events had been woven into their chronicles and traditions in a way that constantly reminded them of what God had wrought. There was a strong sense of continuing activity from generation to generation, and the experience drawn from the past was the ground on which they ventured to hope in God for the present. People sometimes want to sever their link with the past and ignore the legacy of tradition. But Israel knew better than that; and so do we. There are certain events or sayings which always serve to heighten our awareness of nationhood and our moral courage, such as Nelson's famous signal before the Battle of Trafalgar or Churchill's wartime speeches when Britain stood alone. 'We have heard with our ears, and our fathers have told us', that what God has wrought in one generation He may do yet again in a new and troubled generation.

Psalm 45:1-17

*T*HE royal marriage described in this Psalm may have been that of Solomon and Pharaoh's daughter. It falls into two halves which set out the splendour of the bridegroom (45:1-9) and the beauty of the royal bride (45:10-17); and its Messianic significance is made abundantly clear in the New Testament quotation of its key words (45:6-7; cf. Heb. 1:8-9). What of the king? 'Thou art fairer than the children of men; grace is poured into thy lips' (45:2; cf. Song of Sol. 5:10). He is like a warrior girt with majesty, and he rides on his way clad in righteousness. His throne and his sceptre are the symbols of glory and honour; his robes are as sweet as myrrh; music would reflect the gladness that filled the ivory palaces; and the bride would take her place as the queen at his right hand (45:3-9). What of the bride? She is a king's daughter, but her filial loyalties are now to be sublimated in her new life as a king's bride. 'So shall the king desire thy beauty: for he is thy Lord; and worship thou him' (45:11). Desire on his part; homage on her part; possession matched by surrender; a union of spirit which would make these twain one. Then follows the lovely picture of the bride in all her beauty: 'The king's daughter is all glorious within: her clothing is of wrought gold' (45:13, AV). But the *Revised Version* shows that the word *within* refers to the inner sanctum of the royal house in which she was being clothed in bridal array; it provides a contrast with the ivory palaces out of which the sound of music was heard. Raiment inwrought with gold was the fitting attire for her as she left her chamber with the bridesmaids as her escort and came to the palace where the wedding would be celebrated. The king and his bride would rejoice in the prospect of sons and heirs who would clothe his name with honour in all generations (45:14-17). But it is not until we turn to the New Testament that the Psalm lights up with its full significance. It is only 'of the Son' that He said: 'Thy throne, O God, is for ever and ever; and the sceptre of uprightness is the sceptre of thy kingdom' (Heb. 1:8). That royal bridegroom whose glories are divine must be the Lord Jesus, and that royal bride must be the church which has been made meet for the marriage feast of heaven.

Psalm 46:1-11

MAGNIFICENT faith and courage are the pulse-beats in the confident and defiant terms of this Psalm: 'God is our refuge and strength, a very present help in trouble' (46:1). It was undoubtedly composed as a response to some major threat to Israel, but its language is wide enough to allow its application in any crisis situation. The idea of *refuge* is defensive; that of *strength* is dynamic.[1] It is in God that men of faith look for sanctuary, as it is in God that those who are helpless look for succour in the day of battle. The two ideas are caught up in the phrase 'a very present help in time of trouble'. God is more than equal to the gravest emergency: 'Therefore will we not fear' (46:2). This will hold good even though the mountains may shake and the seas be convulsed (46:2-3). And if this be true of the whole created universe, how reassuring for Jerusalem when in a state of siege! There is a strong contrast between the wild turmoil of the ocean and the soft flow of the river whose streams always gladden the city of God (46:4). How then was the Psalmist to speak of that city? 'God is in the midst of her; she shall not be moved: God shall help her, and that right early' (46:5). God had made His presence known in Zion, and the city would not be moved even though the mountains were to totter and fall. Therefore the grand declaration with which the Psalm began is heard again as a slightly rephrased refrain: 'The Lord of hosts is with us; the God of Jacob is our refuge' (46:7). Then the Psalmist calls on us to behold God's work in all the earth: it spells judgement, but the issue is peace, and its object is the glory of God (46:8-11). It is in that knowledge that faith gathers fresh strength and the Psalm ends with the same great refrain. The Lord of hosts is the source of our strength and the God of Jacob is our never-failing refuge (46:11).

---

[1] Kidner, *ibid.*, vol. 1, p. 174.

Psalm 48:1–14

THIS Psalm is steeped in the ardent devotion of a Hebrew patriot whose eyes were ever turning towards the hill of Zion and who rejoiced with all his heart in the God of Israel: 'Great is the Lord, and highly to be praised, in the city of our God, in his holy mountain' (48:1). But the picture needs a larger setting than the earthly Jerusalem; it can only be seen in its total splendour when seen as a picture of that city whose builder and maker is God. 'Beautiful for situation, the joy of the whole earth, is mount Zion' (48:2, AV); her walls and foundations will stand for ever, and the kings of the earth will bring their glory and honour into her palaces (48:3; cf. Rev. 21:24). God had preserved her in spite of threatened calamity (48:4–7): 'As we have heard, so have we seen in the city of the Lord of hosts, in the city of our God' (48:8). Those who kept in mind the loving-kindness of their God would rejoice all the more in what He had wrought (48:9–11). The Psalmist could hardly restrain the spirit of jubilation as he thought of all that Jerusalem meant to Israel: 'Walk about Zion, and go round about her: tell the towers thereof. Mark ye well her bulwarks, consider her palaces; that ye may tell it to the generation following' (48:12–13). Mark ye well! A bold and glorious assertion: 'but the Psalm is not in praise of Zion except as God's abode'.[1] Newton's great hymn caught the point with absolute precision and in terms of sonorous dignity:

> Glorious things of thee are spoken,
> Zion, city of our God!
> He whose word cannot be broken,
> Formed thee for His own abode.

The Psalm rose to a grand climax in the last verse, though it was almost a *non sequitur*: just when one might expect to hear of the crowning glory of that earthly Zion, 'we hear no more of it'.[2] The thought passes from the city of God to God Himself and ends with a glorious utterance whose echoes will never recede: 'For this God is our God for ever and ever: he will be our guide even unto death' (48:14).

[1] Kidner, *ibid.*, vol. 1, p. 181.   [2] *Ibid.*

Psalm 51:1–10

*T*HE fourth and most moving of the seven penitential Psalms reflects a broken and contrite heart in terms with which the meanest sinner may be identified. Godly sorrow as the hallmark of true repentance has never evoked more poignant expression. It is hard to single out one verse in particular from a lament in which every verse is loaded with deep emotional content. The Psalm begins without any form of preface in an urgent appeal: 'Have mercy upon me, O God, according to thy lovingkindness; according to the multitude of thy tender mercies blot out my transgressions' (51:1). Here was David's favourite conjunction of loving-kindness and tender mercy. There was no need for him to name the sin that bowed his head with shame; it was ever before his mind as a filthy stain from which he longed to be cleansed. Grievous indeed was his offence against a fellow man; but even more grievous was his offence against the majesty and holiness of God. How could he rid his soul of that dark blot? There was only one hand that could remove the stain. Therefore he could but plead, 'Wash me, and I shall be whiter than snow' (51:7). Such words reveal the heart of a poet even in that mood of bitter distress. Would that God were willing to make all that was so black white as the snows on Hermon! The Psalm reached the height of yearning in two verses which sum up all that had been said in an appeal of intensified sorrow and desire: 'Hide thy face from my sins, and blot out all mine iniquities. Create in me a clean heart, O God; and renew a right spirit within me' (51:9–10). David spoke for every man when he so spoke for himself; there is no one who may not make that plea his own. Let me take my place on the knees of my spirit with him, and let his words be the cry of my soul in the presence of God Most High!

Psalm 52:1-9

*T*HIS Psalm is linked by its title with the treachery of Doeg the Edomite, one of the most unpleasant of all characters in David's story. Doeg had watched Ahimelech when he allowed David to take the shewbread and to gird himself with the sword of Goliath (1 Sam. 21:7). Doeg came and told Saul what he had seen, and then at Saul's command returned to put Ahimelech and his community to death in a terrible massacre (1 Sam. 22:18). The news of that blood-bath marked the lowest point of all in David's troubles and this Psalm was the voice of his anger at what Doeg had done. 'Why boastest thou thyself in mischief, O mighty man?' (52:1). Doeg the herdsman might ingratiate himself with Saul and take pride in lying slander (52:2 4), but retribution would assuredly overtake him at last: 'God shall... destroy thee for ever... The righteous also shall see it, and fear' (52:5-6). They would laugh at his fall and would speak of him with scorn: 'Lo, this is the man that made not God his strength; but... strengthened himself in his wickedness' (52:7). But there was an abrupt change in the line of thought at this point in the Psalm. David would say no more of that mighty man of mischief; he began instead to reflect on his own sure standing before God in spite of all his troubles. 'But as for me, I am like a green olive tree in the house of God: I trust in the mercy of God for ever and ever' (52:8). Elsewhere the godly were likened to a fruitful tree planted by the waters (1:3), or to one of the palms and cedars which flourished in Lebanon (92:12). But this is a picture of an evergreen olive tree growing in the sacred precincts of the tabernacle. The man who was like that could trust in God's mercy for ever in contrast with the man who trusted in the comfort of his worldly riches. Therefore, dark as was the backdrop, David would end the Psalm on a note that told out his faith in words of praise: 'I will give thee thanks for ever, because thou hast done it: and I will wait on thy name, for it is good, in the presence of thy saints' (52:9).

Psalm 55:12–14

*T*HIS Psalm belongs to a group which had its background in Absalom's rebellion and Ahithophel's disloyalty. Absalom was David's favourite son, and Ahithophel his companion and familiar friend. David could hardly bring himself to think calmly about the course of events inspired by treachery and betrayal on the part of that son and that friend. It was as though God were to hide Himself from his supplication (55:1); his heart was sore with pain (55:4). He was in such distress that he could not refrain from the exclamation: 'Oh that I had wings like a dove! then would I fly away, and be at rest. Lo, then would I wander far off, I would lodge in the wilderness. I would haste me to a shelter from the stormy wind and tempest' (55:6–8). But his restless spirit would have been as restless away in the desert as on the trek to the river Jordan. He felt utterly overwhelmed when he recalled at whose hands it was that all this calamity had come to pass. 'For it was not an enemy that reproached me; then I could have borne it: neither was it he that hated me that did magnify himself against me; then I would have hid myself from him' (55:12). Not the Moabites nor the Ammonites; not those who came down from Egypt or from Edom; not the sons or servants of Saul: their hatred and reproach he could have understood and would have endured. 'But it was thou, a man mine equal, my companion, and my familiar friend. We took sweet counsel together, we walked in the house of God with the throng' (55:13–14). But the thing that made his grief so poignant was the underlying recollection that this was how he had himself acted towards Uriah the Hittite. The counsel of Ahithophel was like that of a man whose words were smooth as butter and soft as oil, but were 'drawn swords' in fact and in intent (55:21). David had no recourse but to cast his burden upon the Lord and trust in Him (55:22–23). But if David were grieved beyond measure at his betrayal by his friend and companion, what must the Lord Jesus have felt at the kiss of Judas?

Psalm 56:1-4

THIS Psalm is set in its historical context by the title which not only ascribes it to David but states that it was 'when the Philistines took him in Gath'. Pursued by Saul, and almost in despair, David had crossed the frontier and taken refuge in an alien court (1 Sam. 21:10). Nothing could have been more ironical than for David to seek safety in the former stronghold of the Philistine Goliath. It was too much for his Philistine enemies; they knew only too well how the Hebrew maidens used to sing his praise: 'Saul hath slain his thousands, and David his ten thousands' (1 Sam. 21:11). He had to feign madness until he could make his escape, and the danger in which he stood found its voice in the first words of this Psalm: 'Be merciful unto me, O God; for man would swallow me up' (56:1). It was as though they were in hot pursuit, and they never let up: 'for they be many that fight proudly against me' (56:2). David had good cause to be 'sore afraid' (1 Sam. 21:12), but the threat to his life only led him to throw the full weight of his need on the mercy of God. There is a graphic touch of realism in the old English phrase in which his faith was expressed: 'What time I am afraid, I will put my trust in thee' (56:3). Though he were to tremble with fear, he would rely in faith on One Who is mighty. That resolve was enlarged upon in the next verse: 'In God I will praise his word: in God have I put my trust, I will not be afraid; what can flesh do unto me?' (56:4). Those words show how faith can transcend man's weakness and distress. The most menacing of his enemies were no more than mere flesh, and what could mere flesh do against one who knew that he was kept by the power of God? The whole verse was taken up and employed as a refrain in the latter part of the Psalm (56:10-11); it was in part quoted in yet another Psalm (118:6), and that Psalm in turn was quoted in the New Testament (Heb. 13:6). Extremes of need in the case of David issued in a triumph of faith which stands for all men at all times: 'What time I am afraid, I will put my trust in thee'.

Psalm 59:1-17

DAVID wrote this Psalm at the time 'when Saul sent, and they watched the house to kill him'. So the title declares, and it accounts for the sense of outrage and the harshness of its language. Saul had sent his servants to watch the house in which David had been lodging, and their orders were to kill him in the morning. But with Michal's warning and help, he was lowered from a window and made good his escape during the night (1 Sam. 19:11-12). There are two main movements in the structure of the Psalm; each movement begins with a vehement indictment of his enemies (59:1-5, 11-13), and concludes with a triumphant expression of faith (59:6-10, 14-17). One verse common to each half of the Psalm reveals the depth of his anger and contempt for his enemies: 'They return at evening, they make a noise like a dog, and go round about the city' (59:6, 14). They were like a pack of snarling dogs on the prowl and in search of prey through the streets of the darkened city. But the Lord would look down through the darkness and would laugh them to scorn. Therefore David could turn in his darkest moment to God as his stronghold and could declare his faith with a boldness that held no fear: 'O my strength, I will wait upon thee: for God is my high tower. The God of my mercy shall prevent me' (59:9-10). God was his strength and would keep watch for him; God would provide for his defence, and that was enough to fill the foreground before his eyes. God was the God of his mercy, and in mercy would go on in advance. There is the strongest possible emphasis of a strictly personal character in the phrase 'my mercy'. The God of all mercy was in particular 'the God of my mercy' and would go on ahead to clear the path and lead the way. It would become almost proverbial to speak of 'the sure mercies of David' (Isa. 55:3). There was glorious certainty in this declaration of faith: it was enlarged and turned into words of praise as the Psalm moved to a close: 'Unto thee, O my strength, will I sing praises: for God is my high tower, the God of my mercy' (59:17).

Psalm 61:2

*T*HIS Psalm was wrung from the heart of David at a time when he was passing through great distress. It may refer to his sorrow for the death of Absalom at the very time when he was returning to his throne in Jerusalem. He poured out his heart in a cry that God would hear his voice and give ear to his prayer: 'From the ends of the earth I call to you: I call as my heart grows faint' (61:2, NIV). No extremity of sorrow or of weakness was so great that he could not cry to Him. But there was more to add, and the same verses extend his plea. It was natural for such emotion to find expression in the language of poetry and metaphor: '...when my heart is overwhelmed, lead me to the rock that is higher than I' (61:2). He felt like a traveller in the desert when the sun beats down and there is neither shade nor water; he longed for 'the shadow of a great rock in a weary land' (Isa. 32:2). What was the rock he had in mind? That rock was the Psalmist's image for God Himself; He is the rock of our salvation, and we turn to Him for rest and refuge. So when the heart is crushed and overwhelmed with sorrow, it will cry out of the midst of pain and anguish: 'Lead me to the rock that is higher than I'. Like a rock, He stands for ever; His love never changes; it cannot be shaken: it is in the shadow of that rock-like love that sorrow-stricken souls find rest and comfort. And though it goes beyond the more immediate point in the mind of the Psalmist, Scripture elsewhere extends the thought of that refuge to the very clefts in the rock (Isa. 2:21). There is shelter from the fierce rays of the sun in the shade of that rock; there is also shelter from the fierce blast of the storm in the cleft of the cliff. Augustus Toplady caught the very spirit of the Psalmist in the words of the hymn:

> Rock of ages, cleft for me,
> Let me hide myself in Thee.

Psalm 62:1-2

DAVID must have composed this Psalm when his troubles were at their height. It is made up of three strophes, each of which begins with the word *only* or *surely* (62:1-4, 5-8, 9-12). The word *only* occurs no less than five times in the twelve verses, and its steady repetition lends a singular emphasis to the bent of his cry. The keynote is sounded in the opening monologue: 'My soul waiteth only upon God: from him cometh my salvation. He only is my rock and my salvation: he is my high tower; I shall not be greatly moved' (62:1-2). David's feelings have been captured by the phrase in the *New English Bible*: 'Truly my heart waits silently for God': it waits for Him with the assurance that in Him our salvation will be secure. God is seen as a rock or a stronghold, favourite metaphors which would reflect the haunts in which David had often found safety. That strong mountain fortress was in total contrast with the idea of a leaning wall or tottering barricade (62:3-4). It was because David had found refuge therein that he was not likely to be shaken. The words with which the Psalm began are then employed to head up the second strophe, but with three mild variations: 'My soul, wait thou only upon God; for my expectation is from him. He only is my rock and my salvation: he is my high tower; I shall not be moved' (62:5-6). David enjoined upon himself the spirit of silent waiting upon God; he spoke of his hope as a solid expectation; and he removed the word 'greatly' from his declaration that he would not be moved. There were times when he did not know how to confide in friends simply because there were no words in which he could express all that was in his heart. But he could wait upon God in silence when words had failed, knowing that God knew all his heart. His faith grew in clarity and in certainty, and it was faith in God *only*.

Psalm 63:1

DAVID poured out his heart in words that would recall his experience in 'the wilderness of Judah'. So the title suggests, and he began with a moving appeal: 'O God, thou art my God; early will I seek thee: my soul thirsteth for thee, my flesh longeth for thee, in a dry and weary land, where no water is' (63:1). He turned to the God of Israel, the God of his fathers, and declared his personal interest in Him with an intensity that could not be ignored. This God alone was God; he knew no god other than Him. Therefore like the watchman who looks for the morning (130:6), he would seek God's face as dawn was breaking. He would lift up his voice in prayer, for his soul was athirst for God. It was as though his whole being were consumed with longing for Him. He would reiterate the same heartfelt longing in a still more striking image: 'My soul followeth hard after thee' (63:8). He pressed after God like Asahel in pursuit of Abner; nothing was allowed to turn him aside. But the picture of that thirst of soul was intensified by the declaration that he was 'in a dry and weary land, where no water is'. He would speak in almost identical terms on another occasion: 'My soul thirsteth after thee, as a weary land' (143:6). But there is no *as* of comparison in the case of this Psalm; his words describe just where he was. He had fled from Jerusalem at the time of Absalom's rebellion and passed over the brook Kidron 'toward the way of the wilderness' (2 Sam. 15:23). This led down to the bleak desert country stretching along the shore of the Dead Sea. It was grim and barren, 'a dry and weary land' that cried out for the rain that seldom fell. David was in a place where there was 'no water' to refresh the sun-scorched desert, and that furnished him with his plea. He was aflame with thirst for God, and none but God could quench that thirst. That taught him to fall back on past experience and to find hope for the future: 'For thou hast been my help, and in the shadow of thy wings will I rejoice' (63:7).

43

Psalm 66:1–20

*T*HIS Psalm begins with a ringing summons that calls the whole world to respond: 'Make a joyful noise unto God, all the earth: sing forth the glory of his name: make his praise glorious' (66:1–4). The Psalm then falls into two halves with eight verses in each, and each contains words of invitation: 'Come, and see'; 'Come, and hear' (66:5, 16). In the first half, Israel was led to see afresh what God had wrought for them as a people from the time when they had crossed the Red Sea until He had brought them into Canaan (66:5–12). Their rich experience of God's mercies was all summed up in a pictorial statement of great beauty: 'We went through fire and through water; but thou broughtest us out into a wealthy place' (66:12). In the second half, the Psalmist narrowed the range of thought in order to pinpoint his own experience as he came to pay his vows in the house of God (66:16). He had come to God in great distress, and his prayer had been turned to praise; and the secret was his total sincerity as he bowed in spirit before One Who is all holy: 'If I regard iniquity in my heart, the Lord will not hear: but verily God hath heard; he hath attended to the voice of my prayer' (66:18, 19). If I cherish the thought of some darling sin in my heart, how can the Lord hear when I cry? If I allow any known sin to lurk in the corner, how can the Lord attend to what I say? Richard Baxter said that 'a sin but once committed is morally continued in till it be repented of'.[1] How well David learnt that lesson! It was only because sin had been put away that he could call upon God with so thankful a heart: 'Blessed be God, which hath not turned away my prayer, nor his mercy from me' (66:20).

---

[1] Richard Baxter, *Works*, vol. xiv, p. 114.

Psalm 67:1-7

*T*HERE is one slight hint in this Psalm which may connect it with a harvest festival. That hint lies in the words, 'The earth hath yielded her increase' (67:6). But that is the only sentence in which the verb is cast in the past tense and the primary emphasis is seen to lie elsewhere. Great as was the joy of fruitful seasons when the earth brought forth its increase, greater still was the joy that flowed from God's blessing on His people. Thus it began with an echo of the Aaronic benediction, 'God be merciful unto us, and bless us, and cause his face to shine upon us' (67:1). Was it that the final blessing at the harvest festival still lingered in the Psalmist's mind and led him into further fields of meditation? At all events, from that point his words turned into direct address to God and the range of his thought began to take in the whole earth. Why should God bestow on them His blessing? It was that 'thy way may be known upon earth, thy saving health among all nations' (67:2). One point of the compass might stand upon Israel, but the other would stretch out to touch the widest circle of all mankind: 'Let the peoples praise thee, O God; let all the peoples praise thee' (67:3). For an ancient Hebrew, that was 'a prayer of great vision', and perhaps of even greater daring.[1] It was hardly enough to speak only of 'the peoples'; it was 'all the peoples' who were to be glad and to sing for joy: for God would judge them with equity and guide them in righteousness (67:4). Then the trumpet call for universal praise was renewed in the same terms (67:5), and the passing mention of a fruitful season served to remind him that there are blessings richer than a golden harvest (67:6). The Psalm changes back from direct address to God in a final definitive statement. The Lord Who brought so much out of little in the harvest increase will make us the means of blessing to the whole world: 'God shall bless us; and all the ends of the earth shall fear him' (67:7).

---

[1] Kidner, *ibid.*, vol. 1, p. 237.

Psalm 68:1-35

*T*HIS is one of the most exuberant of the Psalms of David, and it seems to belong to the triumphal procession of the Ark from the house of Obed-edom to its home on Mount Zion. It was meant to be sung by the white-robed priests and Levites as the journey went on, and the structure stands out clearly as each stage is marked by double spacing in the *Revised Version*. There was a Prologue as the Ark was lifted up on to the shoulders of the Levites, and this begins with an adaptation of the words with which its journeys had always begun: 'Let God arise, let his enemies be scattered' (68:1-6; cf. Num. 10:35). The main body of the Psalm was chanted in two parts as the procession moved forward. The first part would recite the march through the desert while they gradually made their approach to the slopes of Zion (68:7-18), and it reached its culmination with a stirring echo of the triumphant song of Deborah: 'Thou hast ascended on high, thou hast led thy captivity captive; thou hast received gifts among men. . . that the Lord God might dwell with them' (68:18). Those words were caught up by the Apostle Paul and are now for ever enshrined as a glorious picture of the Ascension (cf. Eph. 4:8). The next part would declare how the God Who had redeemed them out of all their troubles would now preserve them from all their foes (68:19-27), and it reached its highest note in words of inspiring poetry: 'They have seen thy goings, O God, even the goings of my God, my King, into the sanctuary' (68:24). The Psalm moved to a close with an Epilogue as the Ark was installed on Mount Zion (68:28-35). The singers, the minstrels, the maidens; Benjamin, and Naphtali, and Zebulun; the princes of Judah and the assembled multitude: they would all join in the final peal of triumph: 'O God, thou art terrible out of thy holy places: the God of Israel, he giveth strength and power unto his people. Blessed be God' (68:35).

Psalm 69:20

*T*HE primary reference of this Psalm must have been to David's grievous sorrows, but the New Testament applies many of its details to the death and passion of Christ. The tone was set with a despairing metaphor in the first words which were reminiscent of an earlier utterance: 'Save me, O God; for the waters are come in unto my soul. I sink in deep mire, where there is no standing: I am come into deep waters, where the floods overflow me' (69:1-2; cf. 42:7). But it rapidly developed into a more objective description when it spoke of those who 'hate me without a cause' (69:4). David was held guilty of wrongs which he had never committed as when Shimei laid Saul's sins to his charge (2 Sam. 16:8; cf. John 15:25). But the key word in the body of the Psalm was the word *reproach*; it is employed five times in the middle section (69:7, 9, 10, 19, 20): 'For thy sake', he cried, 'I have borne reproach; shame hath covered my face' (69:7). He made it clear that that reproach was the very reproach that men had brought against the Name of God (69:9; cf. Rom. 15:3). And the climax was reached in the sorrow-stricken lament: 'Reproach hath broken my heart; and I am full of heaviness: and I looked for some to take pity, but there was none; and for comforters, but I found none' (69:20). Nothing in the life of David can furnish a precedent for the deadly reproach that marked the Cross. They mocked the Lord Jesus with taunts and jibes: if He would come down from the cross, they would believe. They treated with contempt His right to be called the Son of God: let God deliver Him, if He would have Him (Matt. 27:43). He might well have made His own the prophet's lamentation for the fall of Jerusalem: 'Is it nothing to you, all ye that pass by? behold, and see if there be any sorrow like unto my sorrow' (Lam. 1:12). Man's sin was the reproach that broke His heart; for its pain there was no healing. And it was that reproach which caused Him, at last, to bow His head and die.

Psalm 70:1-5

*T*HIS short Psalm is almost identical with the last five verses of an earlier utterance (cf. 40:13–17). It was composed, so the title declares, 'to bring to remembrance', to put God in mind of, His needy servant. It spread before God the circumstances in which David was trapped and which would cry out for God to arise and act on his behalf. David's appeal was so brief and urgent that no words were wasted: 'Make haste, O God, to deliver me; make haste to help me, O Lord' (70:1). That a mere man should call upon the great God of heaven in such abrupt fashion to make haste for his help is a striking witness to the desperate urgency of his situation. David was like a man surrounded by the enemy; he knew that his life was at stake. He could do no more in his own strength and he cast himself on the mercies of God. Let Him confound those who sought after his soul; let Him turn them back as a reward for their shame (70:2–3). The sheer contrast with their malevolent conduct was seen in his concern for the godly: 'Let all those that seek thee rejoice and be glad in thee' (70:4). There was wicked glee in the cry of his enemies: 'Aha, Aha' (70:3); but there was a noble spirit in the cry of others: 'Let God be magnified' (70:4). But then the Psalm reverts to his immediate anxiety: 'But I am poor and needy; make haste unto me, O God' (70:5). There is a variant expression in the earlier parallel: 'But I am poor and needy; yet the Lord thinketh upon me' (40:17). David might be brought low by his many troubles, but he knew that there was endless comfort in the Lord's care for him. But this Psalm did not speak of that comfort; poor and needy as he was, he could do no more than renew the cry for haste. This he did with mingled feelings of confidence and urgency: 'Thou art my help and my deliverer; O Lord, make no tarrying' (70:5). Faith and experience combined to teach him that naught but God could come to his help: so make haste, O Lord, and do not tarry!

Psalm 71:9

THIS Psalm reflects the mind of a man in old age looking backward across the years of a long and full life. There had been the strength and promise of his early manhood; there had been the stir and struggle of his later career. He had been braced and buoyed up all down the years by his faith and he could not refrain from the testimony: 'Thou art my hope, O Lord God: thou art my trust from my youth' (71:5). There had never been a time when God had not been with him, even though this would be to the astonishment of the hostile critic: 'I am as a wonder unto many; but thou art my strong refuge' (71:7). So it was with Moses when he was an hundred and twenty years old: 'his eye was not dim, nor his natural force abated' (Deut. 34:7). So it was with Caleb when he was four score and five years old: 'As yet I am as strong this day as I was in the day that Moses sent me: as my strength was then, even so is my strength now'(Josh. 14:11). And so with John Newton when he reviewed his life in August 1764: 'I am indeed a wonder to many; a wonder to myself; especially I wonder that I wonder no more'. But the years at last had begun to tell for the Psalmist; he knew that he was old and frail. He could feel the onset of weakness and infirmity where once there had been strength. Yet that was not the end of the story. It was against that background of failing strength that he set the long memory of God's never-failing goodness, and that led him to lift up his heart in words of humble appeal: 'Cast me not off in the time of old age; forsake me not when my strength faileth' (71:9). He had been young, now he was old; but he made the weakness of his old age the ground of an appeal to the God Who had been the strength of his soul from his youth. Friends might fail and forget; but God never. God would not let him down in the time of old age nor cast him away when his strength began to fail. He might be old and grey-headed, but the God of his youth was still the God of his old age: therefore it would be his delight to tell of God's grace and might to the next generation (71:17–18).

Psalm 72:5-7

*T*HIS Psalm concludes with a footnote to the effect that 'the prayers of David the son of Jesse are ended': a note that rounds off that series of Psalms of which David was the leading writer (72:20). It was appropriate that his prayers should end with Solomon's succession in view; but its courtly language and its oriental hyperbole look far beyond all human glory or earthly empire. It must be seen as a prophetic utterance which would only find its genuine fulfilment in the Messianic King and kingdom. This is made clear in the central passage which provides a picture of His enduring kingdom in colours of superlative splendour (72:5-7). The King and His people will be bonded in a reciprocal relationship that will last for ever: 'They shall fear thee while the sun endureth, and so long as the moon, throughout all generations' (72:5). Nor do the sun and the moon stand alone in this imagery; the rain and the gentle showers that water the earth play their part as pictures of His benevolence: 'He shall come down like rain upon the mown grass: as showers that water the earth' (72:6). And the effect of that benevolent rule is pictured in the prosperity of His people: 'In his days shall the righteous flourish; and abundance of peace, till the moon be no more' (72:7). It is pleasant to see in these words a definite connection with David's great swan-song at the close of his reign: 'He shall be as the light of the morning, when the sun riseth, a morning without clouds; when the tender grass springeth out of the earth, through clear shining after rain' (2 Sam. 23:4). The whole Psalm ends on a note of ardent worship: 'Blessed be his glorious name for ever; and let the whole earth be filled with his glory. Amen, and Amen' (72:19). Isaac Watts caught up the prophetic intention and the very spirit of this Psalm in his hymn:

> Jesus shall reign where'er the sun
> Doth his successive journeys run;
> His kingdom stretch from shore to shore,
> Till moons shall wax and wane no more.

Psalm 73:23-28

*T*HIS Psalm tells the story of a man who found his way by slow and painful footsteps from overwhelming sorrow to a sure trust in the God of grace and glory. He could not understand the ways of providence; it seemed as though earthly fortune and the dream of personal happiness were quite beyond his reach. He was desperately aware of enemies and aggressors whose one object was to plot his ruin: how was it that they always seemed to prosper while he was left in distress? It was all more than he could bear until he went into the sanctuary of God's presence; then at last he began to perceive the hidden purpose of God. He could address himself to God with an assurance of his interest in God's loving purpose, and the turning point in the Psalm is marked with his declaration: 'Nevertheless I am continually with thee' (73:23). What did this mean? Three things at least. 'Thou hast holden my right hand. Thou shalt guide me with thy counsel, and afterward [thou shalt] receive me to glory' (73:23-24). There was the past: God had taken him by the right hand when he was ready to fall. And there was the present: God would be his guide in all the problems of life. And there was the future: God would make him welcome in the realms of glory. Therefore he could rest with glorious confidence in God Whose love transcends the most unpromising circumstances in our earthly experience: 'Whom have I in heaven but thee? and there is none upon earth that I desire beside thee' (73:25). It was not that human ties were of no account or would cease to matter; but they would lose all their significance if they were thrown into comparison with God. He was frail and mortal, but there was no room for uncertainty or fear. 'My flesh and my heart faileth: but God is the strength of my heart and my portion for ever' (73:26). His problems would vanish as that hope shed its light on his path and the Psalm came to an end on a note of serenity: 'It is good for me to draw near unto God: I have made the Lord God my refuge, that I may tell of all thy works' (73:28).

51

Psalm 77:9-20

THE sad lament with which this Psalm begins points to a man who was close to despair. His doubt and grief were well summed up in the final question: 'Hath God forgotten to be gracious? hath he in anger shut up his tender mercies?' (77:9). But that brought him to the critical turning-point in his reflections on the ways of providence and the very next verse marks the moment of change: 'And I said, This is my infirmity; but I will remember the years of the right hand of the Most High' (77:10). Memories of God's wonders in times of old were the stimulant that faith required in a present hour of trouble. They taught him to recall the fact that the ways of God are always holy and that by them He had made known His strength when He redeemed Israel out of Egypt (77:11-15). That was enough to drown his qualms and to fire his soul with glorious memories of the passage through the Red Sea (77:16-20). He wrote of that ever-memorable event with the freedom of rich poetical imagery. He spoke of the waters as in pain and travail, and the lightning as God's flaming arrows, and the thunder as the roar of Pharaoh's chariot wheels. God had revealed His power over the whole world of nature in terms that the nations could not mistake: 'The earth trembled and shook' (77:18). There was majesty in all that He had done; there was mystery as well: 'Thy way was in the sea, and thy paths in the great waters, and thy footsteps were not known'(77:19). God's way in the storm and on the sea was as sure as always; but His footprints leave no trace in the great waters. 'How unsearchable are his judgments, and his ways past finding out!'(Rom. 11:33, AV). But if men cannot track the ways of God by the measure of their human understanding, they can put their trust in Him as their guide through the deserts of trial and the wastes of perplexity. It is on that gentle note that the Psalm concludes: 'Thou leddest thy people like a flock, by the hand of Moses and Aaron' (77:20).

Psalm 78:67-72

DEREK Kidner suggests that this Psalm could carry the subtitle 'From Zoan to Zion' (cf. 78:12, 68).[1] It is a blunt review of the turbulent history of Israel from their bondage in Egypt to the reign of David. 'It is meant to search the conscience; it is history that must not repeat itself. At the same time, it is meant to warm the heart, for it tells. . . of a grace that persists through all the judgments'.[2] The children of Ephraim were marked out as the largest and most influential of the tribes which made up the northern kingdom. They were condemned as men who had 'turned back in the day of battle' (78:9). Such a terrible indictment points to the fact that their failure on the field of battle was a symbol of their failure to 'set their hope in God' (78:7). This was the cause of their ultimate rejection; God turned to the tribe of Judah instead: 'He refused the tent of Joseph and chose not the tribe of Ephraim; but chose the tribe of Judah, the mount Zion which he loved' (78:67-68). In spite of the glory of Joseph in Egypt and the inheritance of Ephraim in Canaan, God had chosen Judah which had won no glory and Mount Zion which was still an enemy stronghold. God had chosen David as a child of Judah, taken him from the sheep-folds where he tended his flocks, and made him the shepherd of His people Israel (78:70-71). Enough was said with that simple statement of facts, and the Psalm could move to its close with a brief but striking testimony: 'So he fed them according to the integrity of his heart; and guided them by the skilfulness of his hands' (78:72). He watched over Israel as a skilful shepherd would watch over his flock. He brought to that task a singleness of mind and a steadiness of hand that taught him how best to guide and feed them. And that lovely picture of the stripling who was taken from the sheep-folds to become the shepherd of Israel must remain before our eyes as we look to the great Shepherd King Who rules us with perfect integrity and whose skilful hand will never slacken its hold.

[1] Kidner, *ibid.*, vol. 2, p. 280.   [2] *Ibid.*

Psalm 80:1

*I*T is thought that this Psalm referred to the Assyrian conquest of the ten tribes in the northern kingdom. The name of Joseph rather than that of Judah stands in the foreground and is further emphasized by the explicit reference to Ephraim and Manasseh. Joseph therefore stood for Israel as the northern kingdom and its tribes were likened to a flock in the care of a faithful shepherd. But those tribes had been swept into captivity by the Assyrian armies and that explains why this appeal on the part of Asaph was so poignant: 'Give ear, O Shepherd of Israel, thou that leadest Joseph like a flock; thou that sittest upon the cherubim, shine forth' (80:1). That was a *cri du coeur* which would reflect how grave was the shock in Jerusalem at the news from the north and how urgent was their sense of the need for a spiritual return to God. Elsewhere it was the king who had been seen as the shepherd of his people (cf. 78:71–72); but this was an appeal to the mighty God of Jacob as the 'Shepherd of Israel'(cf. Gen. 49:24). Let Him 'give ear'; let Him remember His servant of old; let Him now attend to their cry. And as if that were not enough, it was followed by a further appeal to the God Whose glory shone forth between the wings of the cherubim which stretched above the Ark of the Covenant in the inmost sanctuary of the Temple. Let Him 'shine forth'; let His presence be felt; let His glory appear. And as if that were not enough, it was followed by yet one more appeal: 'Turn us again, O God; and cause thy face to shine, and we shall be saved' (80:3). Let Him turn them again; let Him mark the ascending character of the appeal; let Him observe how it was heightened step by step: 'O God'(80:3); 'O God of hosts' (80:7); 'O Lord God of hosts' (80:19). If He would but cause His face to shine on Judah as it had not in the case of Joseph, they would be saved. Would not the Shepherd of Israel give ear to such a cry?

Psalm 84:1-12

T HE tender and heartfelt longing that breathes through this Psalm was that of a man whose heart was in the house of God wherein he had so often found strength for his soul. The Metrical Version of the Psalms approved by the Church of Scotland lends a special charm to the first verse with its own very personal reference: 'How lovely is thy dwelling place, O Lord of hosts, to me!' (84:1). Was the Psalmist an exile whose memory of the Lord's house filled him with deep nostalgia? And not for the temple alone; it was far more for the living God Whose glory was seen in the sanctuary. Even the sparrow had found a home in its courts and the swallow a nest in its eaves (84:3). More blessed still were those who could dwell in that house and join in the praise of their King and their God (84:4). It led him to think of the pilgrim who went from strength to strength in his journey up to Zion (84:5-7). It was all so remote from where he was in a land of exile, but it fired his soul with longing: 'O Lord God of hosts, hear my prayer: give ear, O God of Jacob' (84:8). Even one day in those courts was better than a thousand elsewhere; he would rather serve as a door-keeper in God's house than dwell like a prince with those who have no fear of God before their eyes (84:10). And if he were pressed to say why he had come to think like this, his answer was in terms of resounding assurance: 'For the Lord God is a sun and a shield: the Lord will give grace and glory: no good thing will he withhold from them that walk uprightly' (84:11). What God gives and will not withhold is all that man in this world can ever desire. Grace is glory in the bud, and glory is grace in its fairest blossom. We stand in grace now; we look for glory to come. It was with this in view that the Psalmist in his lonely place of exile brought his steadfast testimony to a close with words of resolute certainty: 'O Lord of hosts, blessed is the man that trusteth in thee' (84:12).

Psalm 85:1-13

*T*HE text affords no clue to the historical circumstances which lie behind this Psalm, but its literary structure shows that it falls into two halves. First it describes a time of bleak distress through which Israel had had to pass (85:1–7); then it draws a picture of the blessings which the Lord had in store for His people (85:8–13). So it begins with a chastened recollection of past mercies (85:1–3), and one verse in particular stands out: 'Thou hast forgiven the iniquity of thy people, thou hast covered all their sin' (85:2). Nothing could alter their recollection of the mercy that had prevailed with the Lord to forgive all their iniquity and to cover their sin as the waters cover the earth. It was on that basis that he dared to plead the need of Israel in their present situation (85:4–7), and the pleas rise to a climax in the final question: 'Wilt thou not quicken us again: that thy people may rejoice in thee?' (85:6). Nothing could be more in keeping with the character of God as the God of mercy Whose delight is always in the salvation of His people. The Psalm then moves into the next half in terms which reveal how the author himself sought to respond: he would hear what God the Lord had to say, for he was sure that God's purpose was to save all those who feared Him (85:8–9). It was on that basis that he could soar above earthly sorrows in view of the golden prospect held out in God's mighty purpose (85:10–13), and his vision reached a climax in the famous saying, 'Mercy and truth are met together; righteousness and peace have kissed each other' (85:10). It was as though mercy and righteousness were to look down from heaven, while peace and truth sprang up from the earth. Heaven and earth would reach out and join hands with each other, and that bridal of earth and sky would come to its ultimate fulfilment with the advent of the Messianic Saviour. It is in His footprints that His people will tread: 'Righteousness shall go before him; and shall make his footsteps a way to walk in' (85:13).

Psalm 86:1-7

*T*HIS Psalm is the only one ascribed to David in the third part of the Psalter. The Psalm itself has a simple structure; it is made up of three sections. The first and last are an urgent plea for succour (86:1-7, 14-17); while the middle section is full of praise for the God Who is so great and plenteous in mercy (86:8-13). The key is struck in the first verse with its cry at once so plaintive and so urgent: 'Bow down thine ear, O Lord, and answer me; for I am poor and needy' (86:1). There is no clear hint as to the special circumstances which evoked his distress; what is quite clear is that he was in straits, deprived of human aid, threatened by a band of proud and ungodly men. It was the cry of a man who knew how impoverished he had become. His ingenuity and initiative were spent; he could only speak of himself as one who had nothing at all. What could he do? He could only fall back on his experience of what God had done in time past and the very extremity to which he was reduced made him the more willing to throw himself on God's mercy: 'O thou my God, save thy servant that trusteth in thee' (86:2). David's insistent emphasis on his personal interest in God—'O thou my God'—lent a cogent strength and persuasive quality to this appeal which would make it hard to deny. It was in this spirit that his cry was sustained 'all the day long' (86:3); it led to the hopeful expectation that God would yet give him cause to rejoice (86:4); 'For thou, Lord, art good, and ready to forgive, and plenteous in mercy unto all them that call upon thee' (86:5). It was on that basis that he allowed thought to revert to his initial entreaty: 'Give ear, O Lord, unto my prayer; and hearken unto the voice of my supplications' (86:6). His prayer had now gathered strength and he grew in confidence: 'In the day of my trouble I will call upon thee; for thou wilt answer me' (86:7). There was no sign as yet of that answer, but he was sure that he did not call in vain. God would bow down His ear, and would save His servant.

Psalm 87:1-7

PERHAPS this Psalm was written to celebrate the deliverance of Jerusalem after the overthrow of the Assyrian armies by the angel of God (2 Kings 19:35). Jerusalem owed its strength and stability in part at least to its situation on 'the holy mountains' (87:1), but far more to the fact that God had set His love on 'the gates of Zion more than all the dwellings of Jacob' (87:2). The Psalm could not conceal its sense of sheer delight in God's choice of Zion: 'Glorious things are spoken of thee, O city of God' (87:3). The real splendour of that city did not consist in its noble situation on the holy mountains: it could only be seen in those of whom the Lord would say that they had been born there (87:4-6). Zion was to become the grand metropolis for both Jew and Gentile; for the vision of the Psalmist took in Rahab (that is, Egypt) and Babylon, the two rival powers that threatened Israel; the Philistines and the merchants of Tyre, whom Israel had never dislodged; and Ethiopia and Cush, representing countries beyond the reach of the law. Some from among them all would be brought to know Him; their names would be found on the roll of those who were born in Zion. Kidner points out that the Septuagint has an additional word in verse five which was taken up in the *New English Bible*: 'And Zion shall be called a mother in whom men of every race are born'.[1] This seems to have been the origin of Paul's reference to the Jerusalem that is above as the mother of both Jew and Gentile (Gal. 4:26). In that glorious New Jerusalem, the saints of God are all free-born children. The Psalm concludes with a joyous picture: 'They that sing as well as they that dance shall say, All my fountains are in thee' (87:7). The Lord Himself shall lead them like a flock to those fountains all whose springs are in Him, and they shall thirst no more (Rev. 7:17).

---

[1] Kidner, *ibid.*, vol. 2, pp. 315-316.

Psalm 88:1-18

*T*HE tone of this Psalm is one of utter sadness; it is mournful, plaintive, tragic; there is no ray of light, no ground for hope, apart from the moving words of address in the first verse: 'O Lord, the God of my salvation, I have cried day and night before thee' (88:1). It was something that the Psalmist could still think of God as his God and could call on His Name in spite of all. But the Psalm was a long lament for the sorrows which had made life almost unbearable: 'For my soul is full of troubles, and my life draweth nigh unto the grave' (88:3, AV). He would persist in the spirit of prayer, daily stretching out his hands and calling on God (88:9, 13). But he found no relief and was driven to cry with a sense of utter bewilderment: 'Lord, why castest thou off my soul? why hidest thou thy face from me?' (88:14). Yet there was no answer to that cry of anguish; it seemed rather as though a fresh series of blows were to rain down on his forlorn spirit. But the culmination of woes, the grief that caused more pain than all else, was held back until the end: 'Lover and friend hast thou put far from me, and mine acquaintance into darkness' (88:18). So it was in the case of Job: 'All my inward friends abhor me; and they whom I loved are turned against me' (Job 19:19). It was as though he felt that he could bear all the other burdens while his friends stood by him, but he could think of no human ill that was worse than to be cut off from 'lover and friend' alike. Was not this an element in that word of tragedy which fell from the lips of Caesar when he caught sight of his own friend among those who were stabbing him to death: '*Et tu, Brute?*'. But it was to find a darker echo in the haunting cry wrung from the lips of the Lord Jesus: 'My God, my God, why hast thou forsaken me?' (Matt. 27:46). That heart-moving cry, 'My God, my God', was like the Psalmist's address: 'O Lord, the God of my salvation'. That answerless *why* was like the Psalmist's total bewilderment. And that dreadful sense of loss was like the Psalmist's loss of 'lover and friend'.

Psalm 90:1–17

*T*HIS Psalm is thought to have been a prayer of Moses, written perhaps towards the close of the forty years' march through the desert. The Lord Himself is seen as the answer for each homeless generation as men pass down the long trails of time en route to eternity. 'Thou hast been our dwelling place in all generations' (90:1); for 'even from everlasting to everlasting, thou art God' (90:2). There are echoes in the words that follow reminiscent of the watch by night in the camp, or the swollen river which they would have to cross, or the grass so soon dried up and scorched by sun and wind (90:4–6). A whole generation had passed away in the desert as a result of rebellion and unbelief; they had spent their years 'as a tale that is told' (90:9). That grim recollection may have led to the bold contrast between the littleness of time and the vastness of eternity. On the one hand, 'a thousand years in thy sight are but as yesterday when it is past' (90:4). On the other hand, 'the days of our years are three score years and ten; and if by reason of strength they be four score years, yet is their strength labour and sorrow; for it is soon cut off, and we fly away' (90:10, AV). So the longest life on earth is short in comparison with the length of eternity. We live in an age which thinks too little of the brevity of the one, while it thinks not at all of the magnitude of the other. What can be more appropriate for men of time than to bethink themselves of the prayer of Moses: 'So teach us to number our days that we may apply our hearts unto wisdom' (90:12, AV). The man who learns to weigh the things of time on the scales of eternity and to get 'an heart of wisdom' may yet 'rejoice and be glad all [his] days' (90:14); for this will train his eyes on the everlasting grandeur of the God Whose servant he is. 'Let thy work appear unto thy servants, and thy glory upon their children. And let the beauty of the Lord our God be upon us: and establish thou the work of our hands' (90:16–17). His work, His glory; His beauty: perfect wisdom must be to win this for ourselves and our children.

Psalm 91:1–2

THIS Psalm has no title, belongs to no well-known historical context, and is shrouded in all that is anonymous. Kidner observes that its language is sometimes reminiscent of Moses and sometimes of David, and the Septuagint does in fact ascribe it to David.[1] The swift change from the first to the second person, from 'I' (91:1–2) to 'thou' (91:3–13), and the final switch to the first person with a divine speaker (91:14–16), mark the timeless value of the Psalm for all who are in any kind of danger. Nothing can exceed the beauty of the first verse as a picture of the perfect safety of those who put their trust in God: 'He that dwelleth in the secret place of the Most High shall abide under the shadow of the Almighty' (91:1). As the eagle that soars aloft has its secret place in the cleft of the rock, so there is a perfect refuge for those who seek it in the presence of God Who is 'Most High'. Or as a hen covers her brood under her wings, so there is a perfect shelter for the people of God in the shadow of the Almighty. Such a title as that of God Most High will cut every threat down to size, while the reference to the Almighty looks back to the Name by which God had made Himself known to Abraham (Gen. 17:1). Contemplation of his security with God led the Psalmist to commune with himself and to respond in a noble soliloquy: 'I will say of the Lord, He is my refuge and my fortress; my God, in whom I trust' (91:2). It might be said that the secret place and the divine shadow in the first verse are matched by the refuge and the fortress in this verse; and that names like the Most High and the Almighty are matched by the way he went on to speak of *the Lord* and of *my God*. Nothing could be finer than his resolve to trust himself in the keeping of the Lord God. It was in the very spirit of this Psalm that Robert Murray M'Cheyne voiced his ardent longing to draw nearer to God, to dwell beside His heart where love and mercy have their lodging.

---

[1] Kidner, *ibid.*, vol. 2, p. 331.

Psalm 93:1-5

*T*HIS is the first in a group of Psalms which extol the Lord as King. Three of them open with the same thrilling exclamation: 'The Lord reigneth' (93:1; 97:1; 99:1). And the same phrase occurs in one of the other Psalms in a more elaborate context: 'Say among the nations, the Lord reigneth' (96:10). There is no note to tell when this particular Psalm was written or what were the circumstances in view; but the voice of faith rose above storm and tempest with the unshaken certainty that the Lord reigns. All the magnificence of an absolute sovereign belongs to Him as One Who wears the apparel of majesty (93:1). His kingship and glory could only be pictured in terms of the utmost splendour: 'The Lord is clothed with strength, wherewith he hath girded himself: the world also is stablished, that it cannot be moved' (93:1, AV). The Psalm then breaks for a moment into direct address: 'Thy throne is established of old: Thou art from everlasting' (93:2). All this has the ring of jubilant announcement as when the shout of a runner awoke Jerusalem with the exciting news of victory: 'How beautiful upon the mountains are the feet of him...that bringeth good tidings of good, that publisheth salvation; that saith unto Zion, Thy God reigneth!' (Isa. 52:7). But it also has a timeless impact in a cosmic setting: 'For the Lord is a great God, and a great King above all gods' (95:3). Did the Psalm have in mind the cataclysmic events at the time of the Assyrian invasion? Did he compare the might of the terrible Assyrian army to 'the mighty breakers of the sea?' (93:4). No matter; he knew that 'the Lord on high is mighty', and His might is grounded in 'holiness ...for evermore' (95:4-5). The same exhilarating joy pervades Charles Wesley's noble Advent hymn:

> Rejoice, the Lord is King!
> Your Lord and King adore;
> Mortals, give thanks, and sing,
> And triumph evermore.
>
> *Lift up your heart, lift up your voice;*
> *Rejoice; again I say, Rejoice.*

Psalm 95:7-9

*T*HIS Psalm began with a joyous call to worship (95:1-7), but it ended on a note of austere warning (95:8-11). This 'cold douche of realism'[1] was based on the conduct of the twelve tribes at the waters of Massah and Meribah in the wilderness. Early in the desert journey, they had rebelled when they became frantic with thirst and had 'tempted the Lord, saying, Is the Lord among us, or not?' (Exod. 17:7). Again towards the end of that journey, they had cried out with thirst and had provoked Moses to act imprudently (Num. 20:12). God had sworn in His wrath that that generation would not enter into the long-promised rest of Canaan. This was in the mind of David when he came to voice a warning to his generation: 'Today, if ye will hear his voice, harden not your heart, as in the provocation [Meribah], and as in the day of temptation [Massah] in the wilderness, when your fathers tempted me, proved me, and saw my work' (95:7-9, AV). The lapse of time had done nothing to alter the validity of that warning. All that was true in the days of David was still in force when the Epistle to the Hebrews was written. David's words were taken up and quoted no less than five times in the course of that Letter (Heb. 3:7-11, 15; 4:3, 5, 7). They were applied to its readers with the very solemn preface: 'Wherefore, even as the Holy Ghost saith' (Heb. 3:7). The writer looked beyond David to the Holy Ghost as the real author of this warning. It might have been thought that the verb would be in the past tense; but that is not the case. They were summoned to hear the voice of the Holy Spirit as One Who was speaking at that very moment, and Who keeps on speaking. David had applied the lesson to his generation; then this Letter recalled his words as a warning by the Holy Ghost to Hebrew converts in the first Christian century; and we who now read that warning are meant to bring it down to our own age and our own ears. It is more than the voice of a prophet; it is more than the voice of an angel; it is the voice of God Who speaks by means of His Spirit with an authority none can ever gainsay.

---

[1] Kidner, *ibid.*, vol. 2, p. 345.

Psalm 96:1-2

*I*SRAEL was never to forget that one of the great days in their national history was the advent of the Ark to Jerusalem. God had set the final seal on Israel's deliverance from their numerous enemies when His throne was planted in the heart of their most formidable stronghold. David therefore celebrated that great event with the music of trumpet and cymbal, of harp and song. It was on that historic occasion that he chose 'to give thanks unto the Lord, by the hand of Asaph and his brethren' (1 Chron. 16:7). This Psalm, with some minor variations, formed part of the triumphant narrative (1 Chron. 16:23-33). It falls into two halves, each of which is marked by the same ardent response. One half begins with a threefold summons to sing unto the Lord (96:1-6), while the other half starts with a thrice-repeated summons to give unto the Lord (96:7-13). It is impossible not to share in the sheer delight which breaks through the first words: 'O sing unto the Lord a new song: sing unto the Lord, all the earth. Sing unto the Lord, bless his name; shew forth his salvation from day to day' (96:1-2). There would be no room for what was dull or listless or merely formal in that kind of singing; it would grow in volume and quicken in pace with each ardent summons. It called for 'a new song' like the song which the Lord had put into the mouth of the man who had been delivered from the horrible pit and stablished upon the rock (cf. 40:3). It was the song of the redeemed, and 'all the earth' would join in as the choir to sound His praise. What would they sing? They would 'bless his name' and rejoice in His so great salvation which was manifest from day to day. Sing! Sing! Sing! And if the coming of the Ark to Jerusalem was able to evoke such an outburst of song and praise, with what delight shall God's people welcome the day of His return and lift up their voice in the song of Moses and of the Lamb?

Psalm 99:1-9

THIS is the last in the group of Psalms which dwell on the fact that the Lord is King, but there is a different emphasis in the acknowledgement of His sovereign character. Other Psalms in this group abound with sheer delight in His glory; this Psalm moves with measured awe in the light of His majesty and His holiness. It falls into three short sections, two of which end with the solemn refrain, 'holy is he' (99:3, 5); while the final strophe expands that brief phrase yet further: 'for the Lord our God is holy'(99:9). The Psalm begins with a striking picture of the sovereign majesty of God: 'The Lord reigneth; let the peoples tremble... The Lord is great in Zion; and he is high above all the peoples'(99:1-2). Great and awful as He is, all people must learn to praise His name. And why? Because 'holy is he' (99:3). That phrase, stark and simple as it is, was enough to mark how vast is the moral distance of God from man. The Lord is King, and the King's strength is seen in the perfect integrity of all His ways. Therefore the call is to exalt His name and to worship at His footstool. And why? Because 'he is holy' (99:5). This was enforced by the example of Moses and Aaron among the priests and of Samuel among the prophets: 'They called upon the Lord, and he answered them'(99:6). This was never clearer than in the wilderness history when God spoke from the cloud of fire: 'Thou answeredst them, O Lord our God: thou wast a God that forgavest them, though thou tookest vengeance of their doings'(99:8). God forgave Moses and Aaron, though 'their tragic lapse' could not be undone (Num. 20:12).[1] Therefore they could only respond to that call to worship with a chastened sense of humility: 'Exalt ye the Lord our God, and worship at his holy hill' (99:9). The original word order relates this phrase even more closely to the earlier refrain: 'Holy is he... Holy is he... Holy is the Lord our God'. It is like the cry that Isaiah heard from the lips of the seraphim before the throne: 'Holy, holy, holy, is the Lord of hosts' (Isa. 6:3).

---

[1] Kidner, *ibid.*, vol. 2, p. 355.

Psalm 100:4

*T*HE need for a thankful heart is as old as the story of mankind. Memorable occasions for thanksgiving had often occurred in the history of Israel, as when their enemies were overthrown at the Red Sea. There were more personal occasions, as when Hannah rejoiced in the birth of her son. There can be no stronger inspiration for praise than a truly thankful spirit, and this never found more eloquent expression than in the lovely words of the Old Hundredth. Generations of church people have sung this Psalm as the Jubilate in the Morning Service. It is hardly less well known through William Kethe's metrical paraphrase: 'All people that on earth do dwell'. Derek Kidner has observed that 'finer still, but somewhat freer, is Isaac Watts' version, "Before Jehovah's awful throne." '[1] The Psalmist drew a vivid picture of the tribes of Israel as they went up three times a year to the tabernacle when the glory of God shone forth between the wings of the cherubim. In what spirit ought they to draw near and come into the house of the Lord their God? 'Enter into his gates with thanksgiving, and into his courts with praise: be thankful unto him, and bless his name' (100:4, AV). It is hard to resist the warmth of the Prayer Book version: 'be thankful unto him, and speak good of his name'. This was carried over into the New Testament and formed a keynote in the Epistle to the Colossians (cf. Col. 1:3, 12; 2:7; 3:15; 4:2). The very words of the Psalm were quoted in a parenthesis: 'And be ye thankful' (Col. 3:15). Thankfulness represents the feeling of the heart; thanksgiving is the expression of that feeling. And how much there is for which we have cause to be thankful! We count our daily blessings in the world to which we belong or we lift our eyes from earth to heaven as we think of all that God has done. Each of us knows, as no one else can know, how much we owe to His endless care, His guiding hand, His goodness and mercy which have followed us all the days of our life. Then let us be thankful, and speak good of His name.

[1] Kidner, *ibid.*, vol. 2, p. 356.

Psalm 102:1-28

*T*HIS is the fifth of the Penitential Psalms, though it is not so much a lament for sin as the cry of a man stricken by suffering and affliction. The first section (102:1-11) pours out his grief in words that throb through so many of the Psalms: 'Hear my prayer, O Lord, and let my cry come unto thee. Hide not thy face from me in the day of my distress: incline thine ear unto me; in the day when I call answer me speedily' (102:1-2). He was lonely, 'like a pelican of the wilderness' or 'a sparrow that is alone upon the housetop' (102:6-7). He was failing, like a shadow as the sun goes down or the grass that withers before it dies (102:11). The next section (102:12-22) moves on from his private troubles to concern for Zion, and the first words mark the turning-point in his prayer: 'But thou, O Lord, shalt abide for ever; and thy memorial unto all generations. Thou shalt arise, and have mercy upon Zion: for it is time to have pity upon her, yea, the set time is come' (102:12-13). The saints might take pleasure in her stones; they thought that her very dust was precious. But it was not enough to be held in thrall by the past; Zion was to have a glorious destiny in the purpose of God. He would hear the sighing of the captive and would loose the children of death, 'that men may declare the name of the Lord in Zion, and his praise in Jerusalem' (102:21). The last section (102:23-28) goes on to a majestic conclusion which looks beyond all the finite limitations of time to the endless glories of God. The Psalm reverts for a moment to the distress which had prompted the first section: 'O my God, take me not away in the midst of my days: thy years are throughout all generations' (102:24). That was enough; his 'days' and God's 'years' would not bear comparison. It stretched his mind to the utmost and found a vent in a magnificent Messianic statement: 'Of old hast thou laid the foundation of the earth; and the heavens are the work of thy hands. They shall perish, but thou shalt endure: yea, all of them shall wax old like a garment; as a vesture shalt thou change them, and they shall be changed: But thou art the same, and thy years shall have no end' (102:25-27; Heb. 1:10-12). He is the Lord; and He is the same for ever (Heb. 13:8).

Psalm 103:1-22

No Psalm is so exuberant in the spirit of joy and praise as this Psalm of David. He called on his own soul and all that was in him to rise up and bless the Lord. There was vastly more than poetry in this monologue; he drew on the memory of God's infinite goodness to tune all the chords of praise and make them vibrate within. And the keynote was his lively recollection of the forgiveness and the redemption which led him to declare how the Lord had crowned him with loving-kindness and tender mercies (103:1-5). It was clear what this had meant in the case of Israel: God had made known His ways and His acts when He brought them out of Egypt. This paved the way for a virtual quotation of the tremendous utterance in which God had revealed Himself to Moses: 'The Lord is merciful and gracious, slow to anger, and plenteous in mercy' (103:6-8, AV). But the Psalmist did not stop there; he went on to magnify the grace of God by an implied contrast with man's churlishness: 'He will not always chide; neither will he keep his anger for ever. He hath not dealt with us after our sins, nor rewarded us after our iniquities' (103:9-10). He stretched his mind to take in the largest measurements or the widest horizons man can conceive, but they were all far too small to describe the magnitude of forgiveness: 'For as the heaven is high above the earth, so great is his mercy toward them that fear him. As far as the east is from the west, so far hath he removed our transgressions from us' (103:11-12). Therein lies the very heart of this Psalm. God is like a father who has pity on his children because He knows that they are 'frail children of dust, and feeble as frail'. But our sin is only a thing of time while His mercy is 'from everlasting to everlasting upon them that fear him' (103:17). Therefore let the angel hosts and the whole created universe bless the Lord; and let one voice in particular swell that mighty chorus: 'Bless the Lord, O my soul' (103:20-22).

68

Psalm 104:1-4

NOTHING could be finer in vigour and variety of thought and phrase than this Psalm of thrilling worship. It proclaims the greatness of God as seen in all His works, and its structure closely follows the narrative of creation in the first chapter of Genesis. The six days in which God made the heavens and the earth are the key to each successive paragraph of praise (104:1-4, 5-9, 10-18, 19-24, 25-30, 31-35). The Psalm begins and ends, as the last Psalm had done, with the Psalmist's exhortation to his own soul to rise up and bless the Lord with all his being (104:1, 35). Then, without more ado, it set out 'the regal relationship'[1] of God to the world which His hands have made: 'Bless the Lord, O my soul. O Lord my God, thou art very great; thou art clothed with honour and majesty' (104:1). In the words of Robert Grant, He was 'pavilion'd in splendour, and girded with praise'. Then the details follow, 'Who coverest thyself with light as with a garment; who stretchest out the heavens like a curtain: Who layeth the beams of his chambers in the waters; who maketh the clouds his chariot; who walketh upon the wings of the wind' (104:2-3). Robert Grant's great hymn is a match for the Psalmist's lofty range of thought and language as a metrical paraphrase:

> O tell of His might, O sing of His grace,
> Whose robe is the light, Whose canopy space:
> His chariots of wrath, the deep thunder-clouds form,
> And dark is His path on the wings of the storm.

But the Psalmist had more to say before he left this theme, and his words were memorable: 'Who maketh winds his messengers; his ministers a flaming fire' (104:4). This was applied in the Letter to the Hebrews to the angels: they are messengers who speed like the wind; they are ministers who flame like the fire (Heb. 1:7). All this and much more could only prompt an outburst of wonder and worship: 'O Lord, how manifold are thy works! in wisdom hast thou made them all' (104:24).

---

[1] Kidner, *ibid.*, vol. 2, p. 368.

Psalm 105:1-3

*T*HIS Psalm had no title and there is no clue as to the circumstances in which it was written; but, like Psalm 96, it has a special interest in connection with David's bringing up the Ark to Jerusalem. The music and singing in that joyous celebration were long to be happily remembered: 'On that day did David first ordain to give thanks unto the Lord, by the hand of Asaph and his brethren' (1 Chron. 16:7). The first fifteen verses of this Psalm were part and parcel of that celebration (cf. 1 Chron. 16:8–22). It was truly appropriate at such a time to look back and recall the acts of God in their long and chequered national history, and the Psalm was designed as a survey of that mighty chain of events from the call of Abraham to the possession of their inheritance in the land of Canaan. But it begins on the broadest scale in recognition of the manifold providence and care of God for His people: 'O give thanks unto the Lord, call upon his name; make known his doings among the peoples' (105:1). Happy indeed are the people who pause in the pursuit of their daily affairs to share in such national thanksgiving and to make known what God has wrought. The Psalm gathers strength as this call to praise is pursued: 'Sing unto him, sing praises unto him; talk ye of all his marvellous works' (105:2). Few have ever had more reason than Israel and David to sing with all their heart as they proclaim what His marvellous providence has brought to pass. But the apex of that summons is reached in the next words: 'Glory ye in his holy name: let the heart of them rejoice that seek the Lord' (105:3). Such a call to exalt the Lord, to glory in Him, to exult in Him, touches the nerve centre of pure worship; and the call for those who seek the Lord to rejoice in Him goes to the heart of true delight in Him. This is the chief end of man: to glorify God and enjoy Him for ever.

Psalm 107:1-43

THIS great Psalm may have been composed for the feast of tabernacles after the return from exile when Israel was gathered as one man in Jerusalem. This is borne out by the references to 'the redeemed of the Lord' (107:2), and 'the sacrifices of thanksgiving' (107:22), and 'the assembly of the people' (107:32). The Psalm begins with an exhortation to praise for all that God had wrought: 'O give thanks unto the Lord; for he is good: for his mercy endureth for ever' (107:1-3). And it concludes with a splendid picture of the reinstatement of God's people in their own land: 'Whoso is wise shall give heed to these things, and they shall consider the mercies of the Lord' (107:33-43). But there are four intermediate paragraphs, each of which is rounded off with the same refrain: 'Oh that men would praise the Lord for his goodness, and for his wonderful works to the children of men!' (107:8, 15, 21, 31). Each of these four sections is a tableau which provides a different perspective as men view the mighty deliverance wrought by the hand of God, and each follows the same order: human distress, a cry for help, divine deliverance, and the exhortation to praise. The caravan in the wilderness was to discover how God satisfies those who hunger (107:4 9). The prisoner in his confinement was to recognize how God can break the gates of brass and smash the bars of iron (107:10-16). The afflicted in his misery was to understand how it is God Who sends His word and heals those who are at the point of death (107:17-22). The mariner in his storm-ridden vessel was to discover how it is God Who brings him into the haven of his desire (107:23-32). There are countless ways in which men may think of God's mercies. No one knows this better than those who have called on Him out of great distress and have been brought out of all their trouble. Recollection of past distress will be swallowed up in overflowing joy in divine mercy: 'Oh that men would praise the Lord for his goodness, and for his wonderful works to the children of men!'.

Psalm 108:1-5

*T*HE structure and contents of this Psalm are unusual in one particular respect: it was not an original composition, but a happy combination of the closing sections from two other Psalms of David. There are minor variations; but the first five verses were drawn from the words of David at the time when he was hunted by Saul (108:1-5; cf. 57:7-11), and the last eight verses at the time when he was hard pressed by his hostile neighbours (108:6-13; cf. 60:5-12). These two paragraphs, belonging to two different periods, are here combined to make up a Psalm whose buoyant faith and joyous praise are exceptional. The tone is set in the first verse with its declaration of a strong and settled purpose to give himself to praise: 'My heart is fixed, O God; I will sing, yea, I will sing praises, even with my glory' (108:1). Those words may have been wrung from the heart at a time of bleak distress and strain, but he refused to succumb to dismay. He held on to God with a faith that rose above all his troubles; it was rock-like in its resolve, immovable in its purpose. What did he mean when he said that he would sing 'even with my glory'? It was in the very spirit of an earlier utterance: 'To the end that my glory may sing praise to thee, and not be silent. O Lord my God, I will give thanks unto thee for ever' (30:12). He would employ both harp and hymn to praise God with the best member he had; he would awake the dawn itself with songs of praise (108:2). The cave where he had found temporary refuge could not restrict his dream for the future: 'I will give thanks unto thee, O Lord, among the peoples: and I will sing praises unto thee among the nations. For thy mercy is great above the heavens, and thy truth reacheth unto the skies' (108:3-4). Who can measure the height of the heavens or the reach of the skies? And yet greater far are mercy and truth in the glorious providence of God. What could David do but voice the love of a grateful heart in words of boundless delight: 'Be thou exalted, O God, above the heavens: and thy glory above all the earth' (108:5).

Psalm 110:4

ONE of the most striking of all Messianic statements is the central verse in this Psalm: 'The Lord hath sworn, and will not repent, Thou art a priest for ever after the order of Melchizedek' (110:4). Melchizedek had been mentioned briefly in connection with Abraham (Gen. 14:18–20). It is certain that he was no ordinary person: he was the priest of the Most High God and superior to the patriarch who was himself the friend of God. An element of mystery was allowed to surround his name from the outset and it was not relieved until the silence was broken by the Psalmist's declaration. David did not say who he was, but he referred to his priesthood in a remarkable manner. Melchizedek was not only the priest of the Most High; his priesthood was timeless: and the Messianic King was ordained after the order of Melchizedek as a priest *for ever*. This statement was quoted, in part or in whole, no less than five times in the Letter to the Hebrews (5:6, 10; 6:20; 7:17, 21), and there are as well some additional details (7:1–3). He had neither father nor mother, neither beginning of days nor end of life; he was without human genealogy and was made like unto the Son of God. But the climax in that list of facts which marked him out as unique was this: he 'abideth a priest continually' (Heb. 7:3). The word *continually* is in effect synonymous with the phrase *for ever*. Then the author argued that since Christ and Melchizedek belong to the same order of priesthood, what is true of one must be true of the other. The whole argument is based on the assertion that the priesthood of Christ is like that of Melchizedek, and that priesthood is *for ever*. Melchizedek is seen as one who was, and still remains, a priest; he is just as truly a priest now as in the days of Abraham. Only one explanation can account for all the facts, and it is that Melchizedek and the Son of God are identical. The order of Melchizedek transcends the order of Aaron because it abides *for ever*, and the Messianic King like Melchizedek was ordained a priest *for ever*. There can only be one priest who is *for ever*: therefore the appearance to Abraham was a Christophany. Melchizedek was 'like unto the Son of God' (Heb. 7:3), and His priesthood is *for ever*.

Psalm 112:1–6

*T*HIS Psalm is in the form of an acrostic: it has twenty-two lines and each begins with a letter of the Hebrew alphabet. Movement of thought within the Psalm owed more to its literary structure than to formal development of the leading idea: but the leading idea stands out clearly as a verbal portrait of one who is godly. The key is found in the first verse: 'Blessed is the man that feareth the Lord, that delighteth greatly in his commandments' (112:1). To fear the Lord in this spirit is to have that childlike trust and awe which dreads to offend because it is wholly controlled by love. That will make it delightful to obey His commandments and will bring with it the untold blessing of God's favour. Clouds may sometimes darken the sky as Job's experience had shown; but that was not the end: 'Unto the upright there ariseth light in the darkness' (112:4). There are many pitfalls in the path of a man like Job, but the end of that man is peace: 'For he shall never be moved; the righteous shall be had in everlasting remembrance' (112:6). It may not seem like that when men are judged on the scale of earthly values; but scales that are held in the hand of God weigh down with a perfect judgement. They will make one thing plain about that man: 'his righteousness endureth for ever' (112:3, 9). It all fits in with John's vision on the Isle of Patmos. Here is the patience of the saints; here are they that keep the commandments of God. 'And I heard a voice from heaven saying, Write, Blessed are the dead which die in the Lord from henceforth: yea, saith the Spirit, that they may rest from their labours; for their works follow with them' (Rev. 14:13). Their name has been written in the Lamb's book of life; they will not fade into oblivion. They are at rest from their labours, and their work will never perish. Nothing can shake their sure repose; they will be held in everlasting remembrance.

Psalm 114:1-8

ISRAEL was never allowed to forget the grand march of mighty events which had accompanied their liberation from Egypt and their entry into the promised land. Nowhere perhaps was the thrill of recollection stronger than in the terse, vibrant, exciting atmosphere of this short Psalm. That sense of thrill is felt from the outset, even before those events come under review: 'When Israel went forth out of Egypt, the house of Jacob from a people of strange language; Judah became his sanctuary, Israel his dominion' (114:1-2). They had shaken off the fetters of an alien race and a foreign tongue, and they had found a new allegiance in the dignity and the dominion of God. It was as though all the forces of nature had joined in the display of divine intervention. 'The sea saw it, and fled; Jordan was driven back. The mountains skipped like rams, the little hills like young sheep' (114:3-4). It was the hand of God which had made a path through the Red Sea and held back the waters of Jordan so that they passed over dry-shod. It was the hand of God that shook the earth and made Sinai tremble when Moses received the Law. What ailed river and sea, mountain and hills, that they seemed to forget their own proper nature while they succumbed to the power and presence of God? (114:5 6). That series of events was so astonishing, even when viewed at great distance in point of time, that the Psalmist could not refrain from the exclamation: 'Tremble, thou earth, at the presence of the Lord, at the presence of the God of Jacob' (114:7). It is a splendid and awful picture of the mightiness and the majesty of God; but how gracious that this God should be known as the God of Jacob! And that overflowing grace was seen when the same hand that shook the mountains was stretched forth to pour the living waters from the rock and over the sand that they might drink and live (114:8).

Psalm 115:1

THE first verse of this Psalm has a place of its own in the age-long story of all that God has wrought for His people. The Psalm itself reflects the taunts of the heathen and the vehement reaction this called forth from Israel. Those who worshipped idols made of silver and gold looked with contempt on those who scorned idolatry and were apt to ask, 'Where is now their God?' (115:2). Israel's response was bold in the extreme: 'Our God is in the heavens: he hath done whatsoever he pleased' (115:3). The Psalm carried on to exhort Israel, and the house of Aaron, and all who fear the Lord, to put their trust in Him, knowing that He will bless 'both small and great' (115:13). But the tone for this Psalm is set in the splendid spirit of its first words: 'Not unto us, O Lord, not unto us, but unto thy name give glory, for thy mercy, and for thy truth's sake' (115:1). This may reflect some one particular situation in which Israel had looked to God alone for their deliverance. It reads like the defiant utterance of those who had been hard pressed, but who could now give themselves to a triumphant expression of praise as they recalled what God had done. They would take no credit for themselves; they could only reiterate the self-denial: 'Not unto us, O Lord, not unto us'. It is very human for a worldly leader, be it in peace or war, in trouble or prosperity, to set his heart on the goal of what he sees as glory; he seeks fame or renown in the annals of his country as though by his own skill he had brought things to pass. But not so the Psalmist; it was to God alone that the glory belonged; and that glory shone all the more brightly because it was not for any merit of theirs that God had been willing to act. He had done all that He had done for the honour of His great Name and for the sake of His mercy and truth. And the Psalmist voiced his Amen to that grand note of praise in his final declaration: 'We will bless the Lord from this time forth and for evermore. Praise ye the Lord' (115:18).

Psalm 116:12

W E do not know who wrote this Psalm, but the author describes something of the experience through which he had been forced to pass. He could only speak of it in picture language, and the details were not placed on record. But the whole broad outline is there, enough to show that it was a terrifying experience. There had been trouble, sorrow, tragedy, disaster; one calamity had followed another until he was almost overwhelmed. 'The sorrows of death compassed me, and the pains of hell gat hold upon me'(116:3, AV). He began to wonder if he could see things through; he was even in doubt whether he could survive. But at the height of his trouble, he turned to God. 'Then called I upon the name of the Lord; O Lord, I beseech thee, deliver my soul'(116:4). The Lord heard his cry, came to his rescue, and brought him out of his trouble. He was like a man who suddenly discovers that there is solid rock beneath his feet instead of the quicksands of death. He knew that he had been preserved; he was conscious of real security; and he owed it to the intervention of God. His heart overflowed with pure thankfulness and he began to ask, 'What shall I render unto the Lord for all his benefits toward me?'(116:12). This was not a question addressed by man to men, nor was it asked by man of God. It was addressed by the Psalmist to his own heart; he was searching his own soul for the right reply. He offered a twofold answer in the language of poetry, and it is not hard to understand what each answer implies. 'I will take the cup of salvation, and call upon the name of the Lord' (116:13): he would yield all the trust and surrender of his heart in gratitude to God. 'I will pay my vows unto the Lord, yea, in the presence of all his people' (116:14): he would take his place in the congregation and share in the worship of God Most High. There can be no better question for God's people in all ages and all circumstances. Shall our response be on any lesser level than that of the Psalmist? Then what shall I render unto the Lord Who has done so much more for me?

Psalm 118:1-6

*T*HIS was the last of the six Psalms known as the Hallel and sung in connection with the Passover to commemorate Israel's deliverance from Egypt. This may have been the Psalm of the restored exiles when the foundation of the second temple was laid (cf. Ezra 3:10-11). It was also no doubt the Psalm which was sung on the eve of the Passion (cf. Mark 14:26). It is as though one were to hear the voice of a mighty congregation in the identical response to the bidding in each of the first four verses: 'his mercy endureth for ever' (118:1-4). Then a single voice is heard in words of testimony: 'Out of my distress I called upon the Lord: the Lord answered me and set me in a large place' (118:5). The word *distress* is the same as the word used for 'the *pains* of hell' or the grasp of the grave (116:3, AV). The Psalm does not record what that particular distress had been; it was much more concerned to mark what God had done. That led to the ringing reassurance, 'The Lord is on my side; I will not fear: what can man do unto me?' (118:6). Those brave words of faith were taken up and linked with another quotation in the final chapter of the Letter to the Hebrews: 'For himself hath said, I will in no wise fail thee, neither will I in any wise forsake thee. So that with good courage we say, The Lord is my helper; I will not fear' (Heb. 13:5-6). There are as it were two voices: perhaps rather just one strong voice and its heartfelt echo. God speaks to us so that we may speak to Him: His word is rich in love so that ours may be strong in faith. Each word is in the form of an Old Testament quotation, as though the one fitting response to the divine promise (Josh. 1:5; cf. Deut. 31:6) had to be in the words of the Psalmist (118:6; cf. 56:9). God Who spoke in times past by the prophets confirms this word for His people in all generations: it was spoken through them by Him so that faith may teach us how to reply. He will never fail us: therefore we will not be afraid.

Psalm 119:9-11

*T*HIS great Psalm is in the form of an acrostic based on the Hebrew alphabet. There are twenty-two short stanzas with eight verses in each, and the whole alphabet is brought into play as each stanza begins with a fresh Hebrew letter. The grand theme from first to last is the Word of God and, like a peal of bells, the Psalm rings its changes on this theme. The authority and integrity of the written Word of God are viewed from every aspect and are given the most direct application. This is nobly illustrated in the question that stands at the head of the second section: 'Wherewithal shall a young man cleanse his way?' (119:9). Nothing is more necessary for a young man to know than the answer to that question. It is summed up in a single clear-cut statement: 'By taking heed thereto according to thy word'(119:9). What this meant in the mind of the Psalmist is made crystal clear in his own fervent response: 'With my whole heart have I sought thee: O let me not wander from thy commandments'(119:10). He went on at once to apply the lesson to himself: 'Thy word have I hid in mine heart, that I might not sin against thee' (119:11, AV). He had stored his mind with God's Word; it was laid up in his heart; it was cherished in his memory, treasured in his attitude; and it was the safeguard that kept the power of sin at bay. This was never more perfectly exemplified than in the life of the Lord Jesus. His mind and memory were saturated with the text and teaching of the Scriptures. Its words were in His heart and on His lips both in life and in death. It was in the very spirit of the Psalmist that He made use of it in His encounters with the fiercest thrusts of temptation. He met Satan in the stony sun-scorched desert with the threefold word of authority: 'It is written' (Matt. 4:4, 7, 10). Well may we take to heart the words of the Psalmist, exemplified in the life of the Lord Jesus; and make our own Paul's prayer for his converts: 'Let the peace of Christ rule in your hearts...and...let the word of Christ dwell in you richly' (Col. 3:15-16).

Psalm 120:1

*T*HIS is the first of the fifteen Psalms which were known as the Songs of Degrees or Ascents. They became the pilgrim songs of Israel and were sung as the tribes journeyed up to Jerusalem for the three great feasts year by year. They not only came from all parts of the country, but from other countries as well once they had settled there as strangers. This Psalm reflects the start of the journey and the perils that lay in the path of those who came from a far-off land. The place-names and local colour form a vivid background for their anxieties and fears: 'Woe is me, that I sojourn in Meshech, that I dwell among the tents of Kedar!' (120:5). Where was Meshech? Somewhere on the northern steppes whose ruler was an infamous enemy named by Ezekiel (Ezek. 39:1). Where was Kedar? Somewhere in the southern wastes whose people were the implacable nomads of the desert. It was from such distant places, or even from further beyond, that the Hebrew pilgrim had to turn his eyes and bend his steps towards Jerusalem. He was all too aware of the hostile environment in which he found himself; for all too long he had made his dwelling among strangers. He might be for peace, but they were for war (120:6–7). Therefore he could only voice a heart-felt cry to the Lord as he set out for the deliverance the Lord alone could afford. And when he neared the end of that journey, he could only look back with a truly thankful recollection of all the way God had led him: 'In my distress I cried unto the Lord, and he answered me' (120:1). That deep anxiety had wrung from his very soul a *cri du coeur* for divine intervention on his behalf. Nor was that cry in vain; the Lord had heard his prayer. God had cast the mantle of His almighty protection over his head and had brought him on his pilgrim way in perfect safety. Is there any human distress from which we may not cry to Him? And will He not answer in ways that go far beyond all that we may hope or dream?

Psalm 121:1-8

T HIS Psalm would be sung or chanted by the pilgrim bands when at last they caught sight of the mountains round about Jerusalem. The first verse is better rendered as a question with those mountains in view: 'I will lift up mine eyes unto the hills: from whence cometh my help?' (121:1, AV; cf. RV). Thought leapt at once beyond those well-loved hills to the Lord Who is the Maker of the whole created universe: 'My help cometh from the Lord, which made heaven and earth' (121:2). As the mountains are round about Jerusalem, so is the Lord around them that fear Him. There is a break in the *Revised Version* after this verse and the rest of the Psalm widens out in faith and promise. The key is the sixfold use of the words *keep* and *keeper*. Would the Lord ever allow him to lose his foothold? 'He will not suffer thy foot to be moved' (121.3). Would the Lord ever allow him to slip from His mind? 'Behold, he that keepeth Israel shall neither slumber nor sleep' (121:4). All that God was to His people He would be to every pilgrim looking up to those hills and longing for His help: 'The Lord is thy keeper: the Lord is thy shade upon thy right hand' (121:5). The two halves of this verse form a poetic parallel, for the idea of *shade* was a metaphor for the protection which the Lord would provide. Neither sun nor moon, day nor night, would cause distress to the man who knew the secret of that guardian protection, and the Psalm moves to a close with the glorious assurance: 'The Lord shall keep thy going out and thy coming in, from this time forth and for evermore' (121:8). The whole Psalm may be sung to the tune 'Sandon' in the metrical rendering by the Duke of Argyll:

> Unto the hills around do I lift up
>   My longing eyes:
> Whence for me shall my salvation come,
>   From whence arise?
> From God the Lord doth come my certain aid,
> From God the Lord, Who heaven and earth hath made.

Psalm 122:1-9

THIS Psalm abounds in sheer delight on the part of eager pilgrims who had reached the gates of Jerusalem and were ready for their ascent to the place where the Lord had set His Name: 'I was glad when they said unto me, Let us go unto the house of the Lord' (122:1). That was how the tabernacle had been described in the early days of Israel (Judg. 18:31); it may suggest that this Psalm was written while the Temple was yet in the future. At all events, as Kidner says, 'the trials of the expatriate and the hazards' of the journey were now eclipsed by the joy of having arrived at the city of all their dreams:[1] 'Our feet are standing within thy gates, O Jerusalem' (122:2). That long cherished dream would now melt into wonder at the stately city which had risen up so quickly through the genius of David: 'Jerusalem, thou art builded as a city that is compact together' (122:3). But her outward glory was as nothing to her spiritual beauty as the central place of worship for the tribes of Israel. It was there that they came to give thanks to the Lord and to look for justice at the hands of the king (122:4-5). What could be more appropriate therefore than to hear the summons, 'Pray for the peace of Jerusalem: they shall prosper that love thee' (122:6). Kidner points out that 'the sound and sense of the name Jerusalem whose final syllables suggest the word peace (cf. Heb. 7:2) set the tone' of this verse.[2] And its summons for prayer found an answer in the words that follow: 'Peace be within thy walls, and prosperity within thy palaces' (122:7). This went beyond a prayer for peace in view of the threat from warring armies: it marked the longing for peace and concord *within*. It led to the final words of benediction for all who shared with him those ties of sacred kinship: 'For my brethren and companions' sakes, I will now say, Peace be within thee: for the sake of the house of the Lord our God I will seek thy good' (122:8-9). It is for us to lift our eyes like those ancient pilgrims to the glorious new Jerusalem. Our feet shall stand within her gates, and peace shall be within her walls, and the presence of the King will be her everlasting glory.

[1] Kidner, *ibid.*, vol. 2, p. 433.   [2] *Ibid.*, p. 434.

Psalm 124:1-2

DAVID is said to have been the author of this Psalm, and in this case it clearly relates to the days of danger in his early kingdom. There were Philistines in the west, Syrians to the north, Moabites and Edomites in the east: they threatened his borders, marched against his armies, and one by one succumbed to his might in battle (cf. 2 Sam. 8:13-14). Far the gravest of these enemies were the Philistines who had seen the defeat of Saul as an ultimate victory. They had gone up from the coastal plains to hunt and destroy, and had spread out over the valley of Rephaim. David knew that the clash would be crucial: on their part, an all-out effort at conquest; on his part, a bitter struggle to survive. But the Lord Who had helped him in the days of his youth to overthrow Goliath now taught him the tactics he should pursue, and he smote them 'from Geba until thou come to Gezer' (2 Sam. 5:17-25). It was a day he would never forget; nor could he forget that it was only of the Lord that such a battle had been fought and won. 'If it had not been the Lord who was on our side'(124:1). So he began, and then paused a moment to call upon Israel to join in the thunder of that mighty declaration: 'Let Israel now say; If it had not been the Lord who was on our side, when men rose up against us'(124:2). What an *if* with which to begin this Psalm! The Lord had not been on their side when Saul and Jonathan fell on the heights of Gilboa. Had that been the case yet again, David would have been crushed in like manner. And not David only; the people of Israel as well. They would have been 'swallowed up alive' (124:3), 'overwhelmed' (124:4), fatally entangled (124:7). But what were mere men who rose up against them when the Lord was on their side? 'If God be for us, who can be against us?' (Rom. 8:31, AV). The two forces were weighed in the balances; that led to the final jubilant assurance: 'Our help is in the name of the Lord, who made heaven and earth' (124:8). When the Maker of earth and sky is on our side, why should we be afraid?

Psalm 125:1-2

THIS Psalm reflects the mood of a pilgrim who had come from afar only to find the land of his fathers in the thrall of enemy oppression. He had come as it were into his own land, but strangers were in control and the sceptre of the wicked was a heavy burden on the shoulders of his people. But that was not the end of the story; there were hidden sources of strength of which he knew how to avail himself. The hills and the city were still in view and much in mind, and they furnished him with pictures of the divine security to which he clung. 'They that trust in the Lord are as mount Zion, which cannot be moved, but abideth for ever' (125:1). Zion itself has no greater stability than have those who trust in the Lord: they shall never be moved, but shall stand for ever. But his thought went beyond the strength of Mount Zion to take in the encircling protection of God Himself: 'As the mountains are round about Jerusalem, so the Lord is round about his people, from this time forth and for evermore' (125:2). Jerusalem is shut in by two deep valleys and is overlooked from the summit of the hills which lie beyond. Those hills compassed it on every side as majestic guardians of its safety: even so does the Lord bind the girdle of His sovereign protection round His people. When a great host of horses and chariots surrounded the city of Dothan in order to capture the prophet Elisha, his servant was filled with dismay until the Lord opened his eyes. Then 'he saw: and, behold, the mountain was full of horses and chariots of fire round about Elisha' (2 Kings 6:17). Dothan was not Zion; but the Lord would do more still for Jerusalem: 'For I, saith the Lord, will be unto her a wall of fire round about, and I will be the glory in the midst of her' (Zech. 2:5). The mountains round about Jerusalem were like a wall round His people, and would become a wall of fire should need arise to keep their foes at bay. Then well might the pilgrim rest in the strength of that reassurance and voice his prayer with a quiet mind: 'Peace be upon Israel' (125:5).

Psalm 126:1-6

*T*HIS Psalm of six verses first looked backward (126:1-3) and then forward (126:4-6), and the recollection of the past lent it hope and strength for the future. What was it in the past that lit up the uncertain horizon of the future? It was nothing less than Israel's deliverance from the seventy years of exile in Babylon. That was due to divine intervention; they could never feel too thankful. They were delirious with joy; words could hardly express their ecstasy and abandon. It was just like a dream, and the dream had come true. 'When the Lord turned again the captivity of Zion, we were like unto them that dream. Then was our mouth filled with laughter, and our tongue with singing' (126:1-2). Those who recall the vast wave of popular emotion in the streets of Paris or the heart of London at the end of World War Two in 1945 will more readily understand the unrestrained delight of the Jewish exiles. Their grand chorus of praise was heard in the nations around: 'The Lord hath done great things for us; whereof we are glad' (126:2-3). Then what of the future? Memories drawn from the past gave the impetus of hope as they began to look forward. Would that the Lord were to arise and act on their behalf as He had done before! That would be as welcome as when torrents of rain flushed the dried-up water courses of the desert. 'Turn again our captivity, O Lord, as the streams in the South' (126:4). But once that cry was voiced, the Psalm began to melt into quieter tones with its deft picture of the farmer and his harvest: 'They that sow in tears shall reap in joy' (126:5). Their work is hard and may often be heart-breaking; but the joy of harvest will be commensurate. 'Though he goeth on his way weeping, bearing forth the seed; he shall come again with joy, bringing his sheaves with him' (126:6). Costly tears; precious seed; golden sheaves; splendid joy (cf. Jer. 31:9-15). What an encouragement for men in all ages to pray: Turn again our captivity, O Lord!

Psalm 130:1-4

THE sixth of the penitential Psalms begins with the cry of a man who felt himself sinking in a whirlpool of near despair: 'Out of the depths have I cried unto thee, O Lord' (130:1). Imagery like this draws a vivid picture of the terrifying threat of being swallowed up for ever. 'Deep calleth unto deep at the noise of thy waterspouts: all thy waves and thy billows are gone over me' (42:7). But F. B. Meyer rightly observed that 'there is no depth so profound that the soul cannot cry therefrom'.[1] David knew this well in his own experience: 'Save me, O God; for the waters are come in unto my soul' (69:1). So this Psalm poured out its cry for divine intervention: 'Lord, hear my voice: let thine ears be attentive to the voice of my supplications' (130:2). What could have been the cause of such distress? It was nothing less than an overwhelming sense of guilt: 'If thou, Lord, shouldest mark iniquities, O Lord, who shall stand?' (130:3). David wrote from the heart as one who had indeed gone down into the depths. He thought that his sin was concealed; he told himself that no one else would know. The days grew into weeks; the weeks grew into months; and his sin was still unconfessed and unforgiven. Then God sent the prophet Nathan with the story of the rich man who had taken the poor man's one ewe lamb. David's sense of outrage against the wrongdoer backfired. It led to the terrible indictment, 'Thou art the man' (2 Sam. 12:7). Conscience awoke with a frightening vehemence; he now knew that God knew. He could not explain, nor could he excuse. He could only utter that cry from the depths: 'I have sinned' (2 Sam. 12:13). If the Lord were indeed strict to mark his iniquity, he would have sunk beyond recovery. But the Lord put away his sin and his heart rose up in profound relief: 'There is forgiveness with thee, that thou mayest be feared' (130:4). Who is there that may not sink as David did or who does not need to cry, 'O my Father, forgive me, even me; and plant in my heart the tremendous awe and reverence of a truly forgiven penitent'?

---

[1] F. B. Meyer, *ibid.*, p. 253.

Psalm 131:1-3

DAVID is said to have been the author of this short Psalm, and its contents suggest that it must have belonged to his early life as shepherd and minstrel of Israel. It is so free from the sound of strife and trouble that grew up in later years, and so warm in its natural modesty that it seems to reflect his own early manhood when God chose him in place of Saul: 'I have found David the son of Jesse, a man after my heart, who shall do all my will' (Acts 13:22). It was a cry from the heart of a child in love and trust to his father: 'Lord', he wrote, 'my heart is not haughty, nor mine eyes lofty; neither do I exercise myself in great matters, or in things too wonderful for me' (131:1). He knew that pride has its seat in the heart, but looks out through the eyes, and he knew that self-seeking ambition makes it easy to meddle in matters that ought to be beyond one's reach. He would studiously avoid the one as well as the other, and his conduct as a young man in Saul's court bore witness to his amazing discretion in each respect. He was content to wait for God's purpose to be revealed without any sense of fretful anxiety: 'Surely I have stilled and quieted my soul; like a weaned child with his mother, my soul is with me like a weaned child' (131:2). Once a child has been weaned, it no longer craves for the breast of its mother: it was even so that he had learnt to quieten his soul and to hope in the Lord. One may think of Bunyan's shepherd lad and his song in the Valley of Humiliation:

> He that is down needs fear no fall:
> He that is low no pride:
> He that is humble ever shall
> Have God to be his guide.

'I will dare to say', quoth Great-Heart, 'that this boy lives a merrier life and wears more of that herb called Hearts-Ease in his bosom than he that is clad in silk and velvet.'[1] How like David in the lovely springtime of life! 'O Israel', he exclaimed, 'hope in the Lord from this time forth and for evermore' (131:3).

[1] John Bunyan, *The Pilgrim's Progress*, Lutterworth Press, London, 1961, p. 235.

Psalm 132:8-18

PART of this Psalm is an almost verbatim quotation from the words of Solomon at the dedication of the temple (132:8-10; 2 Chron. 6:41-42). Solomon's prayer came to an end with the words, 'Remember the mercies of David thy servant' (2 Chron. 6:42). The Psalm begins with an echo of that closing appeal: 'Lord, remember David, and all his trouble' (132:1, PBV). The trouble in question was an event which had taken place in connection with the removal of the Ark from Kiriath-jearim. It had been left there for twenty years in half-forgotten obscurity until David vowed that at all costs he would bring it to Jerusalem. But his original plan had ended in tragedy and disaster with the death of Uzzah, and the Ark had been left in the house of Obed-edom. Such was David's trouble where the Ark was concerned; but his second attempt was to end in triumph: 'David and all the house of Israel brought up the ark of the Lord with shouting, and with the sound of the trumpet' (2 Sam. 6:15). David placed it in the sanctuary of the tabernacle on Mount Zion and then bent all his strength to plans for the building of a temple. This would be a permanent dwelling-place for the Ark as the pledge of God's presence in the midst of Israel. But the actual construction of the temple and the glory of its dedication was Solomon's great achievement, and the zenith of sheer delight on that great day came when the Ark was placed in the sanctuary: 'Arise, O Lord, into thy resting place; thou, and the ark of thy strength' (132:8). Its journeys were complete and its staves were withdrawn, for it had come to rest in the place where God had chosen to set His Name. It was altogether appropriate that the Psalm should express the longing of Israel: 'Let thy priests be clothed with righteousness; and let thy saints shout for joy' (132:9). The Lord confirmed all that was done; He had chosen Zion: 'This is my resting place for ever: here will I dwell' (132:14). And His answer to their longing was no less plain: 'Her priests also will I clothe with salvation: and her saints shall shout aloud for joy' (132:16).

Psalm 134:1-3

THIS is the last of the Songs of Ascents sung by pilgrims on their journey up to Jerusalem. They had started out from far-off countries like Meshech or Kedar; here they came to an end with the servants who stood in the sanctuary on Mount Zion. Perhaps this Psalm was meant for a pilgrim band which had just arrived; it may have been addressed to those who were about to offer the evening sacrifice. The pilgrims were urgent in their request; it would not brook delay: 'Behold, bless ye the Lord, all ye servants of the Lord, which by night stand in the house of the Lord' (134:1). The tribe of Levi had been set apart by the law of Moses 'to stand before the Lord...and to bless in his name' (Deut. 10:8). They were given a new set of duties once the Ark found its home in the Temple, and some of their number were chosen as singers who were 'employed in their work day and night' (1 Chron. 9:33). They formed a choir which kept up the worship of God throughout the long hours of darkness as well as all day long. It was to the servants of the sanctuary in this night watch that the pilgrims addressed themselves: 'Lift up your hands in holiness, and bless ye the Lord' (134:2, RVM). Lifted hands would be seen as the gesture of prayer; so it had been in the case of David himself: 'Hear the voice of my supplications when I cry unto thee, when I lift up my hands toward the innermost place of thy sanctuary' (28:2, RVM). The same gesture was linked with the act of blessing: 'So will I bless thee while I live: I will lift up my hands in thy name' (63:4). Just so should those Levitical singers lift up holy hands while they blessed the Lord. But that was not the end; there was a glad response to the pilgrim salutation: 'The Lord bless thee out of Zion; even he that made heaven and earth' (134:3). It is a grand picture of those who have come out of great tribulation to stand before the throne of God and to serve Him in the divine sanctuary. They will bless the Lord day and night with songs of never-ending praise, and the Lord will bless them for ever.

Psalm 135:1-18

*T*HIS Psalm has one unique feature: every verse is full of echoes from some other part of Scripture. The cross-references in the *Revised Version* show that it quotes from or is quoted by the Psalms themselves in all but two of its verses. It is like a glorious mosaic in which every verse, or every piece, has its own place to make up the whole. It begins and concludes with a call to praise or bless the Lord in terms of worship (135:1-4, 19-21), while the intermediate verses substantiate that call in three sections which tell of God's dealings with His people (135:5-7, 8-14, 15-18). The first section begins with a reference to the assertion of Jethro to Moses: 'Now I know that the Lord is greater than all gods' (Exod. 18:11). But the Psalmist intensified Jethro's testimony with 'the force of personal conviction':[1] 'For I know that the Lord is great, and that our Lord is above all gods' (135:5). And His greatness is seen in His control of the farthest shining star in the sky or the smallest drop of rain on the earth (135:5-7). The third section throws His greatness into relief by a contrast with the worthless idols of the heathen. They are made of silver and gold in the likeness of men; but they neither speak, nor see, nor hear, nor breathe; they that make them and trust in them are no better than the work of their hands (135:15-18). But the essence of the Psalm lies in the middle section which forms a brief but grand review of what God had wrought for Israel from the time of the plagues in the land of Egypt to that of their inheritance in the land of Canaan (135:8-14). It soars to a climax with a splendid vision for the future: 'Thy name, O Lord, endureth for ever; thy memorial, O Lord, throughout all generations' (135:13). That was the Name which God had revealed to Moses in never-to-be-forgotten language: 'This is my name for ever, and this is my memorial unto all generations' (Exod. 3:15; cf. Ps. 102:12). The God Who had spoken from the heart of the bush that burned with fire and yet was not consumed is the God Whose Name shall endure as a memorial from generation to generation and even for ever.

---

[1] Kidner, *ibid.*, vol. 2, p. 455.

Psalm 137:1-9

*T*HIS Psalm lays bare the pain that wrung the heart of the Hebrew exiles. It is made up of three strophes, and there are three verses in each. The first strophe paints the background by the waters of Babylon, a vast canal system which cut across the plain in a manner totally alien to the hills and valleys of Judea. There they sat and wept as they thought of Zion, and the quiet flow of the waters was a fitting symbol of their dejection. There they hung their harps on the willows that grew by the river, for of what use was a harp when their heart was breaking? And there they were provoked by their captors with the demand that they should sing one of the songs of Zion (137:1-3). The Psalm was to reach a climax in the final strophe with its dreadful imprecation. The sufferings of Babylon would become a mirror of the sufferings it had inflicted on the sons of Zion: 'Happy shall he be, that rewardeth thee as thou hast served us' (137:7-9). But the middle strophe is the very heart of this Psalm as the utterance of a patriot whose soul was on fire with love and longing for his country. Thus it began on a note of defiant loyalty: 'How shall we sing the Lord's song in a strange land?' (137:4). They were exiles in a far-off country; they were homesick for the hills of Zion. It was enough to wring a vow from their lips that sums up all their sorrow: 'If I forget thee, O Jerusalem, let my right hand forget her cunning. Let my tongue cleave to the roof of my mouth, if I remember thee not; if I prefer not Jerusalem above my chief joy' (137:5-6). If their hand were to touch the harp or their tongue to engage in song, let that hand and that tongue shrivel and die. All down the ages men have felt the strength of that pull towards their own country:

> Breathes there a man with soul so dead
> Who never to himself hath said,
> This is my own, my native land!

It may be romantic; it may be steeped in nostalgia. But our homeland is of another character; we look for a better country; it is for that country that our hearts are ever yearning.

Psalm 138:1-8

T HIS is a Psalm of praise in which David's heart overflows with glad recollection of the goodness of God: 'I will give thee thanks with my whole heart... for thy lovingkindness and for thy truth: for thou hast magnified thy word above all thy name' (138:1-2). He spoke out of his own experience; he had passed through a crisis in which he had felt his own total weakness, and his testimony was one of great encouragement for all who are driven to call on God in time of need: 'In the day when I cried, thou answeredst me, and strengthenedst me with strength in my soul' (138:3, AV). Did this refer to that final low point in his early career when he returned to his camp at Ziklag to find that it had been destroyed by the Amalekites? David and his men had lost their all, even their wives and children, because of his mismanagement, and they threatened to stone him in their mood of anger and outrage: 'But David strengthened himself in the Lord his God' (1 Sam. 30:6). In the day when he cried, the Lord heard him, and strengthened him with strength in the inmost region of his being. It was in fact from that very moment that his fortunes took the dramatic upward turn that brought him into his kingdom. Therefore he could write of all his anxieties in the light of after-experience with an abiding sense of thankfulness: 'Though I walk in the midst of trouble, thou wilt revive me... and thy right hand shall save me' (138:7). So it had been in more ways than he could number, and he could look to the future with an unshaken confidence: 'The Lord will perfect that which concerneth me: thy mercy, O Lord, endureth for ever' (138:8). That saying of David was like a staff in his hands for times of need and weakness. It gave him the strength and consolation that God's steadfast purpose alone can afford. All his hopes would rest in those 'sure mercies' which had taught him that the love of God would never relax its hold. Therefore he could conclude on a note of perfect serenity: 'Forsake not the works of thine own hands' (138:8).

Psalm 139:9-10

SMALL thoughts of God vanish like stars before the sun in the light of this Psalm; and yet from first to last it is intensely personal in accent and feeling.[1] David knew that his life had come under the all-searching eye of God, an eye that could see into the inmost recess of his soul. The Lord knew all that was in him better than he himself could ever tell (139:1-5). What then? 'Such knowledge is too wonderful for me' (139:6). It could only prompt him to flee from His presence; but where to go? He might climb the heights; but God is there: he might plumb the depths; but God is there also (139:7-8). But what may seem like a cry of despair soon turned to a superb declaration of faith. David knew all too well the devastating isolation caused by distance and absence from all that is known and loved. He knew what it feels like when a man is called to meet the hazards of a way that he has not trod before. Such a man may feel that it is one thing to know God here; but what will it be like out there? David's answer was as clear as a bell; it was written down in language that is rich in poetical imagery: 'If I take the wings of the morning, and dwell in the uttermost parts of the sea; even there shall thy hand lead me, and thy right hand shall hold me' (139:9-10). Perhaps 'the wings of the morning' point to the vast span of heaven as it stretches from horizon to horizon, while 'the uttermost parts of the sea' was a natural synonym for the farthest point in the west. David knew that God is equal to all extremities; His hand would reach out to guide or hold him in all circumstances. This was made clear in the promise, 'I the Lord . . . will hold thine hand, and will keep thee' (Isa. 42:6). And when He takes our small hand into the grasp of His mighty hand, what is there to fear? David was therefore willing to submit to God's searching judgement with a prayer of profound humility: 'Search me, O God, and know my heart: try me, and know my thoughts . . . and lead me in the way everlasting' (139:23-24).

---

[1] Cf. Kidner, *ibid.*, vol. 2, p. 463.

Psalm 140:1-13

*T*HIS Psalm had its background in the darkest phase of David's experience when he was for ever haunted by the hatred of his remorseless enemies. It is made up of five verses as the beginning and five verses as the conclusion, with a middle strophe of three verses which form the heart of his appeal. The first section is a cry for deliverance from the malice of the wicked; it is a terrible indictment of their violence and enmity. It came to an end with the word *Selah*, a word that would mark a pause in the march of thought (140:1-5). David broke off from that grim train of thought to cast himself altogether on the mercy of God: 'I said unto the Lord, Thou art my God: give ear unto the voice of my supplications, O Lord' (140:6). He may have felt that his cause was at rock-bottom from a human viewpoint, but it moved him to this magnificent affirmation of an unshaken loyalty to God. It was not the only statement of its kind in those black circumstances. The slanders and intrigues of those who sought his life were not hidden from him, but he had clung to the one thing he knew: 'I trusted in thee, O Lord: I said, Thou art my God' (31:14). That strong personal affiance in God now led to an even greater declaration of faith: 'O God the Lord, the strength of my salvation, thou hast covered my head in the day of battle'(140:7). He was so sure of that guardian protection in the heat of conflict because the Lord his God was his strength and his shield. And that cry of faith came to an end with the word *Selah* (140:6-8). The last section was not only a plea that the Lord would not grant the desire of his enemies, but would in fact make their violence the cause of their overthrow. The Psalm comes to an end on the note of undying certainty: 'I know that the Lord will maintain the cause of the afflicted and the right of the needy. Surely the righteous shall give thanks unto thy name: the upright shall dwell in thy presence' (140:9-13). From the day of battle to the glory of His presence: what more could he desire?

Psalm 142:1-7

*T*HIS Psalm belongs to the time of David's flight from Saul to hide in the cave of Adullam (1 Sam. 22:1-2). It was composed at the nadir of his fortunes in a mood of desolate loneliness. There might be four hundred others with him; but who were they? Those who were in distress, or in debt, or discontented; they were almost worse off than he. To him it seemed as if there were no one to take his part; he could only cast all his care on God. There was something like sheer desperation in his lament as he began: 'I cry with my voice unto the Lord; with my voice unto the Lord do I make supplication. I pour out my complaint before him; I shew before him my trouble' (142:1-2). But as he told out his trouble, he summed up his case in words of mingled faith and distress: 'When my spirit was overwhelmed within me, thou knewest my path' (142:3). Just what was his path like? It was full of hidden peril; he felt as though he were friendless; that bleak cave of refuge was a dead-end; and the climax was marked with a sense of profound pathos: 'No man careth for my soul' (142:4). But his very despair of all human support taught him where to look for solid comfort: 'I cried unto thee, O Lord; I said, Thou art my refuge, my portion in the land of the living' (142:5). The Lord was far more to him than earthly consolation, and to that he would cling as long as life was spared. He had been brought 'very low', for those who hated him were so much stronger than he (142:6). 'Stronger than I' indeed; but not stronger than Thou! Therefore he dared to claim that God would bring him out of the prison of his refuge among 'the rocks of the wild goats' (1 Sam. 24:2). He would live to offer his praise to God and to rejoice in the welcome of his people. Shunned and hunted he might be now, but the time would come when crowds would bind their festal garlands as a wreath on their brow because of him (142:7, RVM). The Psalm which had begun at the lowest ebb now came to an end with the tide at full turn: 'For thou shalt deal bountifully with me' (142:7).

Psalm 143:9

THIS is the last of the seven penitential Psalms of David, and it begins with a humbling recognition of guilt. 'Enter not into judgement with thy servant; for in thy sight shall no man living be justified' (143:2). The same terrible awareness of sin has led to a universal desire on the part of men to hide from the eye of God. Such an instinct has been common in all ages and all countries. Adam and Eve sought to conceal themselves from the presence of God among the trees of the garden (Gen. 3:8). Godless men and women will call upon the rocks and hills to fall down and hide them in the day of judgement (Rev. 6:16). Even a child will run away and try to hide when found out in a fault; how much more an adult who has broken the unchanging laws of God? There are things that cannot stand the light of day nor the gaze of men; as a result, we are driven into hiding by our own sense of guilt and shame. Any refuge to screen us from God's eye, to get beyond His reach! As if the eye of God does not see, as if our sin will not find us out? We may hide a great deal from others; they may only see us at our best. We may hide much from ourselves; it is buried in some subconscious area where we hope that it will not come to mind. But nothing is hidden from the all-searching eye of God; He sees all that is in our hearts. How much we need to cry, 'Enter not into judgement with thy servant'. What shall we do? David found the answer; it was the most surprising paradox: 'I flee unto thee to hide me' (143:9). What he could not do for himself, God was able to do for him. He had found a hiding place, a refuge, in God Himself where his sin was covered and his iniquity pardoned. So too we must flee to Him for refuge; we must stand in spirit in the shadow of the cross where our sins were nailed with His hands to the tree. No more fitting prayer can we make our own than the words of Charles Wesley:

> Hide me, O my Saviour, hide,
> Till the storms of life be past;
> Safe into the haven guide,
> O receive my soul at last.

Psalm 144:1-4

DEREK Kidner said that this Psalm has 'a warrior's energy, worthy of David at the height of his powers'.[1] There is no doubt as to its warrior energy, but one may go further and say that it seems to reflect the light-hearted abandon of his earliest forays against Goliath and the Philistines. Those were the days when the daughters of Israel sang his praises in superlative strains: 'Saul hath slain his thousands, and David his ten thousands' (1 Sam. 18:7). The Psalm itself is made up of whole phrases or verbal echoes drawn from elsewhere in the Psalter. Its first verses draw a striking contrast between the strength and greatness of God and the weakness and littleness of men (144:1-4). The very first sentence glows with ardent delight in the Lord Who had made him so strong for battle: 'Blessed be the Lord my rock, which teacheth my hands to war, and my fingers to fight' (144:1). Elsewhere he had written, 'He teacheth my hands to war, so that mine arms do bend a bow of brass' (18:34). But here he dropped the phrase about the strength of his arms and spoke of his fingers which were trained to fight. But how did he think of the Lord? 'My lovingkindness, and my fortress, my high tower, and my deliverer; my shield, and he in whom I trust; who subdueth my people under me' (144:2). Seven titles or descriptive phrases are used for God, and their echoes were loud and clear (cf. 18:2). They throw their own golden light on David as the man after God's own heart, and they prepare for the humbling contrast: 'Lord, what is man, that thou takest knowledge of him? or the son of man that thou makest account of him?' (144:3). David borrowed these words from an early Psalm written to extol the surpassing excellence of God's great Name (8:4). He set them in a new context and had yet more to add: 'Man is like to vanity: his days are as a shadow that passeth away' (144:4; cf. 39:5; 102:11; 109:23). Man is like a shadow cast by a cloud over the sea: it is there one moment; then it is gone. But if God is so great and man is so little, how much stronger was the reason for David to exult in God!

---

[1] Kidner, *ibid.*, vol. 2, p. 477.

Psalm 145:9–13

*T*HIS is the last of the Psalms of David, a glorious finale for the sweet singer of Israel (2 Sam. 23:1), and the last of the eight acrostics in the Psalter. The couplet for the fourteenth letter in the Hebrew alphabet has somehow dropped out of the standard text, but that scarcely impinges on the magnificent tone of praise set in the first verse: 'I will extol thee, my God, O King; and I will bless thy name for ever and ever' (145:1). Praise belongs to eternity, but it reaches down into time and passes from generation to generation. The goodness and greatness of God can never be sufficiently extolled. It could not be better expressed than by quoting God's grand revelation of Himself to Moses (145:8; cf. Exod. 34:6; Ps. 86:15; 103:8; 111:4; 112:4). But David went on to add his own special touch: 'The Lord is good to all; and his tender mercies are over all his works' (145:9). There are countless ways in which the goodness of God reaches out to the least significant of men, and His tender mercy is the glorious canopy spread like an arch over all that His hands have made. The whole created universe joins its voice with that of all God's people to praise His Name: 'All thy works shall give thanks unto thee, O Lord; and thy saints shall bless thee' (145:10). But how shall they tell forth His praise? 'They shall speak of the glory of thy kingdom, and talk of thy power' (145:11). It was altogether appropriate for the royal poet, who had addressed himself to God as his King, to speak of the glory of His kingdom: four times in three verses the word occurs. He broke off his direct form of address for a fleeting moment to dwell on that great theme: 'To make known to the sons of men his mighty acts, and the glory of the majesty of his kingdom' (145:12). Then his outburst of praise rose to its grand climax: 'Thy kingdom is an everlasting kingdom, and thy dominion endureth throughout all generations' (145:13). There was more to follow, but this was the high point of the Psalm. It is for the coming of that kingdom that we are taught to pray (Luke 11:2), and the heartfelt longing of God's people is well summed up in the words of the hymn:

> Thy kingdom come, O God,
> Thy rule, O Christ, begin!

Psalm 146:1–10

THE last five Psalms share the unalloyed quality of praise. Each of them begins and ends with the joyous exclamation, 'Praise ye the Lord'. It is not known by whom they were composed, but they appear to be later than the times of David. The first of the five strikes a chord whose sound reaches from time into eternity (cf. 146:2, 10). The call to praise, common to all five Psalms, is a plural summons, but the very next words show that such an utterance must be personal: 'Praise ye the Lord. Praise the Lord, O my soul. While I live will I praise the Lord: I will sing praises unto my God while I have any being' (146:1–2). Such words carry the echoes of another utterance which has the same sweeping purpose: 'I will sing unto the Lord as long as I live: I will sing praise to my God while I have any being' (104:33). This would lift their eyes far above earthly princes who are often like a broken reed and at their best are only mortal. How much better to look beyond fragile human support to the mighty God of Jacob! Surely no man ever stood in greater need of that mighty God than did Jacob. Twelve times in all the Psalms speak of God as his God, and in this verse for the last time: 'Happy is he that hath the God of Jacob for his help, whose hope is in the Lord his God' (146:5). The Psalm goes on to show what grounds for hope and help that man has whose trust is in the Lord: it is founded in creation and providence, in mercy and judgement, and in ways that surpass all man's finite affairs (146:6–9). Then the Psalmist who would praise his Maker while he had breath concludes with words which not only catch up Zion in their sweep but also stretch on into endless ages yet to unfold: 'The Lord shall reign for ever, thy God, O Zion, unto all generations. Praise ye the Lord' (146:10). Kidner quotes the words of Isaac Watts as the most fitting epitome of the spirit of the whole Psalm:

> My days of praise shall ne'er be past,
> While life, and thought, and being last,
> Or immortality endures.

99

Psalm 150:1-6

*T*HE Book of Psalms moves to a close with a sustained upsurge of praise: a doxology in fortissimo from first to last. It calls for praise in the sanctuary where God's presence is made known and in the heavens where His power is displayed (150:1). It calls for praise in view of His glorious majesty as seen in all His acts and His surpassing excellence as seen in all that He is in Himself (150:2). Nor is that all. David was not only the sweet singer of his people, but the father of church music as well. It is abundantly clear that psalms and songs of praise were set to music. There were elaborate instructions with regard to the instruments to be employed: pipe and harp, trumpet and cymbal, all were part of the Old Testament orchestra (cf. 1 Chron. 13:8; 15:16; 16:5). And the Psalmist called for them all, 'solemn or gay, percussive or melodic, gentle or strident',[1] to accompany this grand final song of praise and worship (150:3–5). This was all in contrast with the purpose which lay behind the use of such instruments at the command of the heathen Nebuchadnezzar: 'At what time ye hear the sound of the cornet, flute, harp, sackbut, psaltery, dulcimer, and all kinds of music, ye fall down and worship the golden image that Nebuchadnezzar the king hath set up' (Dan. 3:5, 7, 10, 15). But the noblest use of music is in the praise of God Most High. The tradition of centuries now lies behind the use of an organ for this purpose. The word itself is found four times in the *Authorized Version* (Gen. 4:21; Job 21:12; 30:31; Ps. 150:4). But this is a mistranslation; in the *Revised Version* the word is always rendered as a pipe; it was closely linked with the harp. The pipe was the favourite wind instrument and the harp the favourite stringed instrument of Israel. Both elements are combined in the instrument we now describe as an organ, and an organ is designed to provide for a richer volume of full-throated worship. So the Psalmist would have us draw out all the stops in a mighty outburst of praise: 'Let everything that hath breath praise the Lord. Praise ye the Lord' (150:6).

---

[1] Kidner, *ibid.*, vol. 2, p. 491.